# Th[...]

# Attraction

## *for*

# Love

MW00398774

# The Law *of* Attraction *for* Love

*The Secret to Finding Your Soul Mate*

DEBBIE FRANK

Ulysses Press

Published in the U.S. by Ulysses Press
P.O. Box 3440
Berkeley, CA 94703
www.ulyssespress.com

First published as *Debbie Frank's Cosmic Ordering Guide to Life, Love & Happiness* in 2007 in the United Kingdom by Penguin Books

ISBN10: 1-56975-634-1
ISBN13: 978-1-56975-634-8
Library of Congress Control Number: 2007905468

10 9 8 7 6 5 4 3 2 1

Printed in the United States by Bang Printing

U.S. proofreader: Amy Hough
Editorial assistant: Lauren Harrison
Production: Lisa Kester
Interior design and layout: what!design @ whatweb.com
Cover design: TG Design
Cover photos: portrait of a smiling woman ©Image Source Pink/Alamy;
    Take My Rose ©iStockphoto.com/Kyu Oh

Distributed by Publishers Group West

To James and Lulu Mei—
you are my very special deliveries!

# Contents

# Introduction

What if…you could attract anyone and anything into your life simply by thinking about it and intending it to happen? Well you can! The Law of Attraction for Love is so strong that you have the power to re-think your entire life! Yes, it's entirely possible for you to create whatever you want. You can bring a soul mate into your life, you can put an end to a series of dead-end relationships, you can change some bad patterns that make an existing relationship unhappy. You won't even have to learn anything new, because the fact is that you are already harnessing and using the Law of Attraction every single day of your life. Yes, every person, situation, and experience is there as a result of how you've been thinking. Your thoughts constantly dictate the quality of your life. The universe is a mirror of what you've been thinking. So if you'd like to up the quality or even quantity of your relationships then all you have to do is think better thoughts. Re-direct your mental energy into positive, happy pictures that radiate out from you and attract the good things and the good people your way.

So often we think that life just happens to us—it's fate, it's karma, it's someone else's decision. It's so easy to forget that actually **this is your life** and you alone have the power to make the choices, to change your life any way you want. You're the one in charge—no one else. If you worry all the time about never meeting anybody, or re-live bad times with previous partners either in your own head, or discussing them with others then you're creating more of the same energy around you. If you feel stuck in a situation, then it's come about as a result of what you've been thinking. In other words, it's not the universe's fault because it's only delivering to you exactly what it hears you talking about. Your core beliefs get lived out, so if you are afraid deep down that there's nobody out there for you, or that love affairs are dangerous, unpredictable and often end badly, then that's what you're going to get. Sometimes we don't even realize that we believe these things because they're buried deep, and we are telling ourselves at the same time that we do want to meet Mr. or Miss Right, that we are in fact looking for a true love. We're conflicted about the whole nature of love. So that's what we get—conflict!

As soon as you get it straight in your head about what kind of love you desire and intend to have in your life, that's when the universe can get to work on your behalf. If you expect great things and great people then that's what you'll get. You can work out how wonderful life would be if you had no limits, if anything was possible. It is! There is no difference between what's going on "out there" and what's going on "in here." It's all the same: We attract whatever we think about most, so it's an inside job!

The wonderful thing is that you can begin right now, no matter what your history is. Whether you've been married five times before, or never at all, whether you want to re-vitalize the love you once had for each other, or simply enjoy dating, this book is for you. The time is right. You can change your whole life in a moment if you change your thinking right now.

The Law of Attraction for Love centers around the magnetic energy of our expectations. You are a magnet that draws things to you. Whatever you have in your life comes to you via the Law of Attraction. So it's important to expect what you want and never focus on what you don't want. How many times have you said to yourself "I'd really like X to happen, but it probably won't." We say it to ourselves to try and cushion any disappointment, but the universe just hears you saying it probably won't happen and surprise, it doesn't! This book is a tool for making you aware of just how much power you have and hold. Your life is what you create, so you can start over right now. Nothing is ever wasted, so every experience and relationship you've had has prepared you for this point. You can start now. You can make the Law of Attraction for Love start working in your favor. It's never too late.

As an astrologer my clients often ask me, "What's going to happen to me?" The question implies that the cosmos has it all mapped out for you. People are taken aback when I reply, "What do *you wish* your future to be?", *because eventually you become what you think.* Our thoughts are incredibly powerful—they are like viruses that spread so rapidly that they have an impact on everything we do. How we think not only influences events in our lives, but also determines how we experience these events, what we attract, and what we make of it all.

So if what we're thinking is such a big deal, then it's essential to think the right thoughts. If we think positively then we can actively use this amazing facility, this ordering device, this delivery service. We can request all sorts of things—an opportunity, a relationship, a greater sense of happiness. This doesn't have to be an ego trip either—you can also ask for someone else's happiness, or wish them well in life. But is it really going to work? Can a wish make a difference? So often I hear people say, "I never meet anyone. I never get offered what I want." What's going on? This book will reveal why you've got the power to change everything.

# ARE YOU READY TO USE THE LAW OF ATTRACTION?

You are the one who holds the power. We are constantly emitting a vibration, a frequency that's determined by what we're thinking at any time. When you come back from vacation your mind feels clearer, you see what's important in your life and what's not; you know what you want and are ready to go after it. If you can return your mind to this positive, happy holiday state as often as possible then you're going to attract all the good things and good people to you.

# ARE THINGS MEANT TO BE?

So, are things "meant to be"? Does fate deal us a hand? To a certain extent, yes. We are not blank slates. We come in with some things already written, yet it's what we chalk up that counts. We can't choose what we are born into (or maybe we can, but that's another spiritual theory). We can, however, always choose what we think and how we deal with things.

If a solid object, such as a spoon, can be bent using the power of the mind, then reality isn't nearly as stable or immovable as it looks. Everything is in the process of change at some level. We can choose to think the thoughts that lead us to happy, successful relationships. *We interact with fate all the time*. Sometimes we think of ourselves as powerless to do anything, and that's when circumstances dictate what happens. Sometimes we block things. We try to take control and then we get in the way of the wonderful Law of Attraction. We don't have to control anything—just focusing on love and believing in it, brings it.

# WISH

I wrote this book because I believe that there is more to the Law of Attraction than simply making a wish. *You are the vital ingredient, the one who holds the power. You need to* ***start practicing the art of the possible.*** In this book you'll be able to work out your relationship patterns, see what's blocking you from having a relationship, learn about how you can think differently, act in a powerful way and make your wishes reality. I have experienced the extraordinary way The Law of Attraction works in my own life. It led me to my husband James who is 12 years younger than me. It took a lot of emotional lessons, letting go and signaling from the universe before I was finally open enough to receive someone different from my agenda. When it came to becoming a mother, I hoped against hope that it would happen and tried every medical intervention possible. But it was the Law of Attraction, divine intervention, which made it possible for me to become a mother to our daughter Lulu-Mei, adopted from China. She is the perfect soul for our family, defying biology and genetics to prove that the strongest links that bind us together are all about love and the Law of Attraction. This book has come into your hands, whether by choice or by "accident." You can start creating the love that you want right now. I hope the secrets of the *Law of Attraction for Love* will bring you greater love and happiness.

# CHAPTER 1

# The Universe– Two Worlds Colliding

## THE VISIBLE WORLD

Is it what it's cracked up to be? What nobody tells you is that what we're seeing isn't necessarily what we should believe in. We each have a different take on life, love, and the universe. We see things through our own perspective so that no one else's reality exactly matches ours. Physically, things look the same, so we assume they are the same. For example, a plate is a plate. But even these objects are not as solid as they might at first appear. They are made up of tiny vibrating particles that hang together in a shape that we see and touch, and understand to be a plate or a cup. All things in our physical everyday world, including the food we eat, the clothes we wear, and our own bodies, are all made up of the same stuff—energy.

If we accept things at face value it means our vision is limited, restricted, less than it could be. We don't get beyond appearances. We are also fed the scientific view:

that something can only exist if it is proved. In the medical profession any cure that has not been proved in scientific conditions is called "anecdotal evidence" and assumed to be false even if it has brought about recovery. If we apply this kind of mindset to another aspect of life, then it's amazing that we are able to experience love—because it cannot be proved! Clearly many things that cannot be proved and therefore "don't exist" have enormous value, are a powerful force in our lives and mean a great deal to us.

The extraordinary thing is that no scientist has been able to prove that the so-called "real world" actually exists. The world looks real enough, but under microscopic examination it turns out to be a force field of raw electromagnetic energy that arranges itself into shapes and patterns that we recognize and that register in our brains as various identifiable objects.

So you could say that we manufacture the world inside our heads, because our bodies and brains receive messages and our five senses organize impressions about what's out there, and we process the information into our nice, old familiar world. Ah, there it is again. We repeat the sights, sounds, and signals to ourselves and are reassured that we still exist, that everything is still there and is still the same.

Except it isn't.

The real wow factor to come out of all this is that we create our own reality and we choose to see what we want to see. We each shape and choose our own version of reality through individual filters, which are our qualities as human beings, our expectations and our environment.

What wonderful liberation! It means that we are not limited to experiencing life as "what happens to us." The universe is in fact a reflection of you. You can change or rearrange it into a shape that suits you.

Now this might sound as if it requires a magic trick, or years of yogic discipline. But actually there is nothing unusual about it. You already do it. You are already seeing the world through your own views, ideas, tastes, conditioning, and awareness. And it looks very different to you than it does to the next person.

# THE INVISIBLE WORLD

There is an invisible world that infiltrates every aspect of our being. This world is what glues everything together, connects us to everyone, and helps us make sense of life. It contains our feelings, our hunches, our knowledge, our connections with others. It is what Jung called "the collective" and what Deepak Chopra calls "the soup."

Some people feel more connected to this invisible realm than others. Doctors, scientists, and engineers tend to be fascinated by what they see in tangible terms in the visible world, while media types, artists, and writers will often be drawn to the invisible. But, putting that aside, we are each of us positioned somewhere on the spectrum and we shift between the two extremes.

There isn't very much difference between what we see "out there" and what is going on inside us. The physical world fools us into thinking we are all separate and disconnected, and that what we're looking at or encountering in life has nothing to do with what we are thinking or feeling on the inside. Yet so much of what really goes on is invisible. Our thoughts, which are the governing body of our entire life's experience, cannot be seen. So we don't think of them as having so much power. We live in a "lookist" age, one in which how we look and physically appear is given so much importance that it's hard to remember that so much of what makes us unique and individual lies underneath the surface of what we see. In fact, as much as 99% of you is invisible. How you feel, what you're hoping, thinking, imagining, your memories, your past, even what's going on in your body is not necessarily on display to the outside world. We are forced to live in the "real" visible world because we have been born into it. We live in our body; it is our first home. Dealing with the physical is an essential ingredient of life. We all have to accept the inescapable real world: dealing with money, finding a place to live, getting food to eat, sleeping, moving and existing within our physical selves and environment.

The invisible world, on the other hand, is optional—some people live in a state of denial about their feelings, try not to think too much and choose "not to go there." They value fact over imagination, material goods over love. The invisible realm is where love comes from. It's a place of infinite possibilities where we find guidance, inspiration, kindness, acceptance, and forgiveness, and also our sense that something big is about to happen. If we repress or deny this invisible realm, our feelings get totally blocked up, creating a vortex of negative energy.

The invisible realm gets a lot of knocks from the hard-core, real-world fraternity. As if it doesn't exist. Which is fair enough because it's invisible! But just wait until one of these rational types of people falls in love. Then they realize that there is more to life than facts and figures. But, of course, the scientists have got their hands on love too, recently announcing it is no more than a bunch of chemicals being released into our bloodstream. They say we are really at the mercy of a quick hit of serotonin or love hormones. This may be true at a biochemical level, but it's also the spiritual-emotional, out-of-this-world feel-good factor that connects two souls, and love cannot be reduced to the level of a few hyped-up chemicals on the loose.

# GOOD OR BAD?
## REALITY IS NOT OBJECTIVE

The invisible realm joins us together. When clients come to see me as an astrologer and I start explaining about a particular transit of a planet on their chart, they will often interrupt and demand to know, "Is it good or bad?" This sums up how disturbing it is for us to embrace any invisible force without us immediately wanting to organize it—before it's even happened—into something manageable and definable. That's how we take control. Or we think we do.

What happens to us shouldn't be categorized in this way, because out of the worst experiences comes the most awareness, and the surfacing of inner strength. Sometimes the "good" experiences that we look forward to, such as marriage or the birth of a baby, can also be the most stressful. Nothing is as it seems or as it is expected to be. It is all just part of the whole—it just **is**; it's the law of nature.

Every situation can be viewed as good or bad depending on who's doing the viewing. In fact, this either/or mentality can be extremely wearing. Every time we judge, we reduce our possibilities and opportunities. This is the kind of attitude that can lead to division, divorce, and even wars. So just when you're about to attack someone with all the force of an emotional terrorist, it's good to remember that each of us is made up of the same stuff (visible world), and that we are all connected (invisible world).

No matter how separate, isolated, or lonely you feel, whether you choose to go off and meditate in silence in a mountain hut for twenty years or lie in bed all day with a migraine, it is simply impossible to be disconnected. *You are part of the soup whether you want to be or not.*

Whether you choose to have your closest friends on speed dial or not is entirely up to you. Having people available to you through the five senses and technology gives you a presence of sorts. But spending time seeing, talking to, or exchanging emails with people is not the only way to maintain a connection or bond.

A baby learns that his parents still love him and will care for him even when he is alone at night in a crib. He has to develop a trust in the invisible world—for example, with the help of a transitional object, he is able to hold on to the love of his parents even when temporarily they are not present. If we had never learned this then we would literally be tied to our mother's apron strings well into our mid-life crisis.

The truth is that we often connect with one another through thought alone. Thinking of someone immediately puts them in the front line of the Law of Attraction. Don't you sometimes think of someone and they call you?

# ENERGY

Which brings us to energy. By that I don't mean food calories, or what you expend on the treadmill or by running after your child or lover. I mean the energy that is the stuff of life in the invisible realm and is the very thing that we pick up on without even realizing it.

This kind of energy comes in different weights and forces. It can be felt as a heavy force that lumbers around like an elephant, towers high as a skyscraper, or fills the air in the form of a black mood. In contrast, light energy can be like fine cotton, a feather, or a kiss.

We feel the energy of another person even though it's invisible. It's what attracts us to particular people, makes us move away from others, and in some cases (if we are especially permeable) can allow us to take on the moods of others and then wonder why we feel the way we do. You must have noticed there are some people who carry with them a very dense, heavy energy—we feel it as soon as we are around them. It's an air of negativity that fills the atmosphere and can try to invade us too if we don't protect ourselves from it. There are other people who radiate out a happy energy that is equally infectious—we feel good around them, we are lifted, and feel good about life in their presence. (The ultimate trick to using the Law of Attraction is to consciously radiate this feel-good factor whenever and wherever you can, because the universe is honor-bound to deliver to you more of the same!) Feeling the energy, the mood, the atmosphere, the vibration—whatever you want to call it—requires you to notice and pick up on the subtle forces and currents that swirl around places, people, and situations. The Law of Attraction is an energy supplier that you tune into and pick up on. You can imagine connecting to this force field, like being connected to the national power grid. You switch on, you connect to the force.

The more you are aware of this energy, the easier it is to understand what's going on, time your moves, and begin to work with the Law of Attraction.

## HOW WE CAN CHANGE THE ENERGY OR THE EXPERIENCE

Since the world arranges itself around our expectations, we can make a difference in it by changing them. For instance, if you expect a particular person to be difficult, self-pitying, greedy, selfish, or demanding, then that is exactly what they will be. But if you see them each time you meet as if for the first time, with fresh eyes and zero expectations, then you are giving them the opportunity to surprise you. Our expectations determine what we get every time. So you hold the power to change what you're getting from someone simply by altering what you're looking for.

Nothing and no-one gives out a constant energy vibration—it's all a matter of how we look, see, and receive that object or person. In fact, I could go as far as to suggest that the mere fact of our presence in a room filled with objects would change the energy of that room. That the minute we observe something it will be changed by who we are and what kind of energy we bring into the room. Bring two live people together and we get a far more combustible energy. Our "chemistry" with another person is created by the vibrations we're giving out mixed with the ones they're giving out.

Imagine the power you have at your fingertips for making your dreams real when you tune into the Law of Attraction for Love. We are asking for something or someone in a spiritual sense; we're dipping into universal intelligence, but what and whoever we receive will be earthly. Whatever we attract to us is a result of the connection we make between heaven and earth, the divine and the mundane, what we wish for and what we are capable of receiving.

# UNDERSTANDING THE UNIVERSE IN TERMS OF THE LAW OF ATTRACTION

It's important to open your energy channels and to be receptive, aware, and available to receiving signals from the invisible world—both those we receive from other people, and those we pick up on confirming that we are on the right track, in the right place, or on to something.

The whole point is not to be asleep on this great journey called life, but to be alert to the messages that are available. To make sure that you are conscious of what you want to attract, and awake for the delivery, no matter what time it comes.

You need to notice your own energy, your life force. Become aware of the ebb and flow, and of how much impact certain people and situations have upon it. How can you reinforce your energy and protect yourself against energy-sappers? You need to be strong in body and mind, bright-eyed and bushy-tailed in order to receive the best life has to offer.

The whole process means that you can't afford just to sit back and let life happen to you. Sure, there are confusing energetic currents out there that could cause you to drift from time to time. But you need to steer a course, and have a purpose, a love, or a destination in mind. Saying yes to life means making sure you're aware of and using everything that's available to you.

You must have heard about the self-fulfilling prophecy, when someone voices his anxiety and his worst fear comes to pass. Whenever you feel down, or are worried, you immediately put a stop to the flow of energy. In fact, there is a great deal of truth in the saying that you are your own worst enemy. Every time you think a negative thought, assume the worst, or buy into any group mentality that's operating on fear, you lose the bright energy that attracts love. The media is constantly telling us bad things, making us worry that our lives are in danger and that disease, death, and disaster are around the corner. Media thrives on drama–it sells newspapers and grabs our attention, but without realizing, we are drawn into operating in fear mode. You might want to choose more carefully what you listen to and what you read rather than just switching on the (bad) news in the morning. It's simply not conducive to feeling good— and the more you radiate out good, happy feelings, the more love you're going to generate in your world.

If you fixate on problems, they often seem much worse. You begin by thinking one stressful thought and suddenly everything feels bad. That's not to say that thinking or talking about "bad" things will always create negative energy. It's true that a problem shared can be a problem halved. But it can also mean a problem doubled! If you can come through those thoughts or conversations with something positive, or if you can help someone through positive listening (but not magnifying), then you are opening yourself up to good energy, to solutions, or to a feeling of release.

## THE CONCEPT OF ABUNDANCE AND FLOW

Never hesitate to give of yourself freely. Be generous with your love, ideas, and gestures of kindness. Giving of yourself is the greatest gift you can give to other people. This means being present rather than distracted, and really listening rather than thinking of something else. The more you love life, other people, and yourself, the more love surrounds you. You will never run out of the great spark of love, and the more you give, the more you can manifest. Out there in the invisible realm is enough raw energy and love to create whatever you are capable of imagining. So don't be stingy when it comes to giving it out.

You also need to be generous and kind to yourself, which means making your own happiness a priority and relaxing where possible. Not chasing after things, running around, or trying desperately hard. If you take the effort out of doing things it means that the flow can be restored. Worrying yourself silly that you won't find the right person, or you will never fulfill your desires, or things won't work out, only clogs up your energy system and creates the expectation that you will lose out. This is dangerous. **Being happy is the number one magnetic force for attracting love.** If you can summon up feelings of happiness no matter what is going on around you, you've discovered one of the key factors in changing your life for the better. What's interesting is that the universe is listening to you whenever you complain and will hear it as a request for more of the same! The greatest antidote to difficulty is cultivating a positive attitude, whatever life throws at you. Make sure that you've got some happiness reserves inside you that you can dip into at any time. These will quickly reverse any negatives that are spinning around. Know what it is that makes you happy in the smallest of ways. Then you can instantly inject a little happiness into your life and create an upbeat mood by something as simple as listening to your favorite music. You can become better at being happy by trying to experience it in small pieces rather than expecting 100% happiness all the time. A good little trick is to appreciate all the good things you've got in life. Don't forget that as soon as you feel good you're tuning into the magic of being able to receive more good experiences and good people. It's as if you set your frequency to receive good things. And the more you give out the more you get back. Every time you think something negative, it sends out a blocking energy on something good happening. Now why would you want to do that?

If you don't have the love you want right now, it's because deep down you are blocking yourself from having it. And the reason other people have love in their lives is because they've radioed out the right thoughts and the right person has received them. All you have to do is tune into the right frequency, transmit feelings of love outward, believe it's possible to have this love, and to conjure up in your mind the good feelings you associate with it.

Since the Law of Attraction forms such a key ingredient of your life experience, once you realize how much power you've got to magnetize love into your life you'll want to use it all the time. The clearer your thoughts and desires, the easier it is to harness. In the next chapter you will discover just what the Law of Attraction is and how the universe can respond.

# CHAPTER 2

# What is the Law of Attraction?

## WHAT IS IT?

The Law of Attraction is simply the way in which you draw various people and life experiences to you. This force exists even without you realizing or doing anything, but in order to make it work for you in a more positive way it's good to build up a better relationship with this force/flow of energy/ infinite intelligence so that your wishes and desires can manifest. Working with the Law of Attraction requires intention, belief, a desire to break patterns from the past, and the capacity to spot and take advantage of opportunities. The law operates on thoughts, words, and actions— these are the messages you're putting out, and the universe simply mirrors them back to you.

# IF YOU WANT HELP

The universe is non-denominational and does not mind what you call it or how you communicate with it. All that matters is that you are able to fully focus on your desires and hopes, really believe in them 100%, and be open to how they might be delivered (which may not be in the form you imagine).

# WHAT IT IS NOT

This may all sound wonderful: that you can ask to date a never ending supply of gorgeous people or dream up the perfect lover. The Law of Attraction is also the means by which you could zoom up to the top job and become one of the A-list. If you want this to happen strongly enough and believe in it powerfully, it can work for you. But the Law of Attraction should be seen as a dynamic tool to help you transform rather than as a universal supplies store and mail-order delivery service.

This universal energy cannot be used to harm other people, to take away someone else's free will, or to get what you want at someone else's expense. It is essentially a benign influence that can be tapped into.

Nor is the Law of Attraction a panacea. For instance, it can't magically make you recover from a serious illness. There are many occasions where people have gone into remission through sheer willpower or positive thinking—

but that's another book in itself and I wouldn't want to make any sweeping statements suggesting that this process can right the world's wrongs. It is simply a way of tuning into the best available opportunities for you.

# FATE AND FREE WILL

Is our life determined by fate or free will? Do we determine our lives through the use of willpower, and are we totally free to do so? Or does fate lend a hand—do we have a destiny that is born the moment we first draw breath? I like to think of life as an interplay between fate and free will. We are all born with a set of building blocks that's unique to each of us. Yet what we choose to build with them, and what we make of our lives, is our decision. On the other hand, we sometimes experience certain events and relationships as having an element of fate about them. That "love across a crowded room" syndrome—is it fate, or the Law of Attraction? Is it "meant to be," the hand of the daimon, or do we contribute to our own fate by attracting various situations and putting out specific signals?

Where does fate begin? When the chromosomes arrange themselves so that we are destined to lean toward certain qualities and characteristics? Some spiritual thinking argues that we choose our talents, our childhood conditions, and our relationships before we are even born.

But, even so, there may be scope to change the experience via free will.

# HOW TO USE THE LAW OF ATTRACTION

The truth is there is no "correct" way to do it. But whichever way you do choose to communicate with the universe needs to fit in with your beliefs and feel right for you. You might want to meditate, listen to music, write down your wishes in a private journal, or say them out loud like a prayer. You might have a special time of the day or a particular place that feels still and quiet enough for you to sense the connection with this force field or universal energy. But you don't have to sit cross-legged, burn incense, or become a yogi to do it. If you feel like placing one of your desires while driving, or as you push a shopping cart around the supermarket, that's fine. The important thing is that you do it in a heartfelt way. You can even visualize sending a desire like you would send a text or an email. (This can also work with unwanted thoughts that get stuck in your head—just press the delete button!)

## THE GOLD STAR LAW OF ATTRACTION SERVICE

Timing is notoriously difficult—the universe doesn't necessarily respond with a same-day delivery. But you can boost your chances by practicing with gold-star intentions. This is a highly concentrated version of the standard kind. It involves putting in your desire with a much greater degree of passion and conviction. So instead of idly thinking, "It would be nice if such-and-such happened," you actively engage yourself with the process 100 percent, body and soul. You don't just make a wish, but you visualize yourself having already achieved whatever it is you desire. You see yourself having/being/doing your wish in the present tense. Feel what it is like to already be with this person, to be part of a couple, or to have met "the one." This intensifies the vibration. If you are able to radiate out the perfect vibration of what you want then the perfect people will be attracted to you.

Strangely, the universe seems to know whether you expect to get what you want, or whether you have a sneaking suspicion that you won't, or whether you're wondering if you really deserve it, or if it's not possible at all. Every time you lose a bit of hope or belief that your desire will be delivered, the flow of energy drops and you get stuck in the waiting game, unable to be supplied with what you want. The whole process requires you to be 100% behind it.

I was made aware of the non-verbal cues that deliver messages of intention when I signed up to do a morning at the horse school, which is part of the Miraval Spa in Arizona. Most of my group had no previous experience, but we were each assigned a horse to groom and school. First, as we watched the instructor show us how it was done, it seemed easy, and his horse obligingly responded to everything he wanted it to do.

Then it was our turn—starting with cleaning up our horses' hooves. I was handed the tool to do the job, and my horse was tethered facing in the opposite direction. So how could I get this horse to pick up its foot? That's when I realized that I was at a total loss as to how to make this animal do what I wanted it to. Words were useless. Showing it the tool, touching its leg—both generated no response.

As the instructor came around he told us to move toward the horse's leg with conviction. To stop doubting whether the horse would cooperate. He asked us to imagine the horse responding perfectly and to hold the picture of this happening in our minds. Animals (like people) pick up all the nonverbal clues: they get their instruction from your body language, and will take no notice if you fumble and act as if you don't know what you're doing. The moment I held the intention more powerfully, abracadabra, that hoof came up to be cleaned.

I learned from that little episode that how you hold yourself and convey your intentions really does matter. The universe, like the horse, also responds to clear intentions better than to maybes. A big breakthrough in your mission to get your desires met is to act as if it has already happened. Then you will adopt the posture, the mind set and the emotional responses that go with the fulfillment of that wish. And, as energy attracts energy, you're more likely to get your desires and intentions delivered. You can expect gold-star service if you're putting in gold-star intentions, without misleading information, doubts, or confusion. The more committed you are, the easier it is to get what you want.

How many times have you heard someone say, "I had good intentions, but..." Unless you keep the outcome in mind then the energy for it just slips away, disappears, and evaporates into the nothing.

## BECOMING A MAGNET

Actually, this heading is a misnomer, because you already are a magnet. Without realizing it, you attract everything into your life by virtue of who you are and by what you are thinking, imagining, speaking about, and doing. The universe is always reflecting yourself back to you, so what happens to you is a mirror of what you've been thinking and feeling, what you've been worrying about, or how positive and upbeat you've been. To a great extent character is destiny. We are constantly creating vibes that draw experiences to us.

It's so easy to think that you're not responsible for what happens. And in some cases clearly you are not. But in the free will versus fate debate you have take a 50-50 hit and at least own up to being involved in the process of generating your life experiences. Some people like to think of themselves as scriptwriters choosing to invent line character or love interest. We do have the power to create "instant karma", in which our actions sow the seeds of the outcome.

## KEEPING OUT THE NEGATIVE

It's always important to keep visualizing what you want, instead of running worst-case scenarios through in your head. If you are continually fixating on not having something or someone then the energy is sent into a spiral and has nothing to do except send you more of the same. The vibes you send out when you don't love yourself actively pushes people away; it's a repelling force. You can change how you feel immediately by changing what you're thinking about. **You need to know that you deserve to have love. Expect to receive it.** Remember, whenever you are worrying, as far as the universe is concerned you are making plans—so stop that immediately!

It's also important to learn how to protect yourself from other people's negative vibrations and from the general garbage that's out there. It's so easy to be put off by those who ridicule you, or who secretly don't want you to get what you want. Why don't they want you to move forward? Because you then undermine their own position, and they may have heavily invested in life staying the same. If you meet the right person, or become much more fulfilled and happy, in their eyes you will leave them behind. Don't take their feelings personally, by the way. That's great protection in itself.

## WHEN THINGS FEEL RIGHT

If we open ourselves up to noticing the little signals in the universe then we'll see when our desires are confirmed. Someone we know will lend us the book that tells us more about what we want to do, or we'll read an article "by chance" that helps us make the next move. We feel good about our choices and wishes from gut instinct or sudden inspiration right through to their eventual outcome.

## ACTIVE WAITING

Successfully working with the Law of Attraction for Love requires you to actively wait, rather than passively wait. What this means is that you fully intend to get a result, but are aware that you need to read the signals, currents, timing, and conditions and make adjustments as and when necessary. The right person for you might come in a different package from the version you are imagining.

This is different from simply waiting—which means giving up your own will and power, and handing over responsibility to the universe to deliver. Just staying in and expecting the right person to knock on the door is not going to get you anywhere. Using *intention* is like exercising a muscle—you need to go to the mind—gym and practice using it in your everyday life in order to make it stronger.

# WHEN THE UNIVERSE FAILS TO DELIVER

What if you've put out your intentions and desires for the love of your life and the universe hasn't sent one recorded delivery, or you weren't available for signing when the courier called, or you feel your desire has simply gone astray in the mail? Does that mean that you won't ever get meet "the one"? That you should give up, because the Law of Attraction doesn't work? This is when you might start asking yourself if you're meant to be alone forever, or suffer a string of losers or painful relationships. Is this all there is? Is this it for you? Or are you sabotaging your own chances? Maybe deep down you feel you don't deserve love, or you're not ready to commit yourself to being with someone. Chapter Six shows you how to shift any blocks which might be preventing your wishes from being fulfilled.

# ARE WE ENTITLED?

Obviously we are not entitled to get whatever we want with a snap of the fingers. We can also get fixated on and obsessed about our desires. We can't stop thinking about a person; we are compulsively drawn to the idea of being with someone. We are so attached to this desire that we actually block off the flow of energy and, we lose our ability to relax. Being so uptight about it puts the flow of energy into reverse. We demand that the universe delivers and satisfies our ego as if it is our right to have whatever or whomever we want. But it doesn't work that way.

Sometimes you want something, or someone, but it simply isn't the right time for it to happen. You sometimes have to let go of the time frame and allow the universe to get on with delivering at its own pace. Or maybe you've asked for something and don't realize that the universe has acknowledged your wishes and is trying to fulfill them, but you can't recognize it because the outcome isn't exactly what you had expected. In this case, maybe your specifics need a rethink. Perhaps it's time to break out of old relationship patterns and open up to being with a different kind of person. If things aren't happening for you, then maybe you need to change. The same goes for trying to attract a wonderful job or home. We might need to think laterally, change career, or consider re-locating.

We need to recognize when some effort on our part is required. But there is a lot to be said for simply relaxing and trusting that the universe will do its best to deliver what you want, subject to stocks, availability, and the absolute rightness of your intention—i.e., whether or not it will fit into the grand scheme of things. Sometimes it's good to follow the Law of Least Resistance. Which means opening yourself up to what the universe is trying to bring you and going with the flow, so there's less struggle. Extending your search parameters to focus more on the quality of you want, rather than its material substance, is a brilliant way to get the Law of Attraction to work for you. If you focus on your desire to be powerful rather than attracting a CEO then it's an order that the universe can fulfill in whatever way is possible.

Inevitably you cut yourself off from a lot of good possibilities by being very picky or too specific about the details. Also, dare I say that maybe we don't always know exactly *what's* good or right for us. The important thing is that you are able to harness that magnetic energy or attraction and direct it toward the kinds of things or people that will enhance your life.

# YOU DON'T HAVE TO MANAGE THE PROCESS

Developing trust and a positive attitude isn't as easy as it sounds because we live in a world that appears to operate on the need to be in control. You can even say that trying to harness the Law of Attraction for Love is an attempt to maintain a degree of control. But there is always a mystery X factor—we can't control everything in our lives. There is a mysterious process at work that introduces us to some experiences and some people, but not to others. We're back to the interplay between fate and free will. But we can assume that the universe has some kind of intelligence, that there is meaning in what we encounter, and that we don't live a totally random life full of chaos and incidents that are slung together without any coherent intention.

For instance, we may spend a lot of time wondering how we can be with X if he or she is already with someone else. Or how we could go to Fiji if all our funds are already allocated. But the more uptight we get in trying to arrange everything and work it all out, the more stagnant the energy becomes. Don't waste your time asking yourself how it could possibly happen. We don't need to know, we just need to believe! We need to be able to fall back into the flow, relax, take it easy, and let the universe in its wisdom relieve us of the burden of working it out.

We don't have to resolve all the issues or try so hard to make it work. We don't have to bash our heads against a brick wall. We can be more Buddhist in attitude and serenely accept our current situation, while hoping for the best and thinking positively. We don't have to make a snatch-and-grab raid on what we want or the person we'd like to be with, or continually fight off the competition, or struggle so hard. If we can get into the flow then our whole energy changes. We can just focus our attention on expecting love to come our way and stop getting so engrossed and involved in the details that send us into a negative spin. Sometimes we are so wrapped up in the specifics of a problem, that it feels impossible to resolve. Sara thought she had her love life sown up when she married 33-year-old Steve. He checked all her boxes, was good looking, successful, and nice. When the marriage broke down she found herself at age 36 with her biological clock ticking very loudly. After a lot of in-between relationships and soul searching, Sara thought she'd never realize her dream of a happy family of her own. Sara dropped her dreams, stopped trying to get a series of attractive playboys to commit, and concentrated on being happy in herself. When she was 39 she met Josh, a widower her age with 2 gorgeous boys. Now Sara is happily married to Josh, a much loved stepmother, and expecting her first baby too. It just goes to show sometimes we can only solve problems by letting go and getting out of the rut. We outgrow the problem; it is no longer a big deal.

# BEING AWAKE AND ALERT

Being awake and conscious is a crucial element of successfully attracting what you want. If you go around half-asleep and don't really notice what's going on in your life and what it's all about, then unsurprisingly, it's hard for the universe to get through to you. You might be asleep when the messenger calls! And you might be so sound asleep that you even fail to register what your nighttime dreams have to say to you, which is often a key way that inspiration comes.

It's not like just putting in a positive thought is going to overturn something that is deeply ingrained in our lives. We need to look at what we're all about and the messes we've got ourselves into, and understand that successful fulfillment of our wishes may require us to change our attitude toward life. In other words—it's not totally up to the universe. We need to be personally involved, accountable, aware, and ready.

☀  ☀  ☀

In the next three chapters I'm going to focus on the Law of Attraction for love and relationships. For some of us love seems like the hardest thing in life to find—but that's all about to change.

# CHAPTER 3

# The Attraction Factor

## THE LAW OF ATTRACTION FOR LOVE

### WHO ARE YOU ATTRACTING—AND WHY?

What is it that draws two people together? Is it fate or pheromones? Is it as simple as making a choice? Is it love at first sight? A compulsion or an unconscious pull? Is it really possible to bring someone into your life by thinking the right thoughts and putting out your intentions? Or to make a relationship better by changing the way you think?

If we are to realize why certain people come into our lives, or don't as the case may be, then we need to understand what's going on beneath the surface. We need to discover what we are magnetizing, and what it is about us that keeps pulling in or pushing away particular people.

**The first step is to ask yourself:**

What are you putting out?

What are you getting back?

And what links the two? Do you keep attracting the same kind of person?

What is your secret agenda?

## WLTM (WOULD LIKE TO MEET)

It's easy to say you *would like to meet* someone. But what kind of person? What do you really mean? Dating websites and personal ads are full of people that seemingly want the same thing. GSOH (good sense of humor) seems to be a must, as is being fit, solvent, and single. But if it really were that simple, and people were so easy to please, then why do so many of us find it so difficult? Scratch the surface of your WLTM and you'll find a whole different agenda.

Are you desiring total oneness, openness, togetherness, acceptance, support, and connection of souls, all in glorious blazing technicolor, with flashing lights and sexual attraction?

Are you addicted to longing for the wonderful future person, or the ex who got away?

The more you distract yourself with dreams of the future or memories of the past, the less energy there is available for the here and now. The addiction to longing can also be a hard one to break. Maybe we enjoy feeling that our ideal relationship is in the future, that Mr. or Miss

Right will come along one day, and in the meantime the hidden pay-off is that we fool ourselves into believing that we're not afraid of intimacy, so we can avoid dealing with a real relationship.

---

Do you feel let down by the endless disappointment?

Maybe you never get lift-off?

Are you in a long-term relationship that fails to deliver its promise?

Or have you had a series of no-hopers: a pattern of people with different names and faces, who purport to being unique individuals, but end up blending into one distinctive theme in your life?

---

The amazing thing is that the similarities between these no-hopers doesn't really have to do with them, but with you! You are doing something to attract this kind of person. As they say—once is chance, twice is coincidence, three times is enemy action! Meaning there is something going on in your unconscious that invites this pattern, or this type of person, whether you realize it or not.

# YOUR RELATIONSHIP PATTERNS

Has someone got their hooks into you? You're in a tricky relationship that makes you feel unloved. Maybe you don't even realize that this is a pattern for you, but on some level deep down you pick up what's happening. It goes something like this: You don't feel very connected, understood, or loved in the way you would like to be loved by your mother or father. Then you find yourself with someone who you have instant attraction with. The person treats you badly and your inner unconscious blueprint tells you, "Here we are again, that's very alluring and very attractive, I recognize it, it's familiar, I'm at home with this one." Of course, rationally it's not what you want.

But astoundingly, if we have a wobbly attachment to our parents we tend to recreate it in later life, simply because it feels familiar. So our attraction factor would go something like this: "Oh yes, this person makes me feel insecure; I recognize this feeling from my childhood; this absence of positive love feels familiar; I'll go for it." It looks crazy on paper. And of course you might be busy telling yourself and your friends that you're really looking for love, but underneath you're attracted to the lack of love that you have experienced before.

Suzie had a very difficult relationship with her father; he was often away from home on business when she was young and had very little time for her when he was around. She experienced him as being critical, cold, and emotionally absent. Yet when Suzie met a high-flying guy who traveled a lot with his job, her unconscious attraction factor was working overtime. The whole pattern was repeated as Suzie struggled to get close to this guy who didn't really have any time for her, and turned out to be very withholding. It took a while for her to see the light, to see what she was doing by going for the familiar. But when she did, she was able to move on to a more rewarding relationship.

Then there's compulsion. When we feel instantly attracted, the power of the feelings are huge, but they are not necessarily going to generate a positive relationship. The symptoms of compulsion are a lack of freedom over your *choice*. Even having a "type" implies that there is some kind of hook or pattern at work that operates without you really choosing.

Unhooking yourself requires you to say no to the habitual and to consider what you really want and need. To become aware. Give yourself some space to examine the pull before choosing. What is it? A big build up of desire energy? Or an old pattern overlaid with desire and compulsion? That instant chemical reaction might be good information that someone is a possibility for you, or it could be a hook that plays havoc with your biochemistry in the same way addiction would. You go unconscious, forget to spot the warning signals to take things slowly, or to ask yourself if this is truly, deeply what you are desiring. The key is to be discriminating, and at the same time remain open.

# THE MESS IN THE MESSAGE!

We need to understand the effect our upbringing had on us. Carl Jung and Sigmund Freud's take on our neuroses is rooted in what happened to us in early life. Whether we feel we had a normal, ideal, or difficult childhood, this belief has lot to say about the potent image of our parents that we carry around in our psyche.

Even if our parents are long dead, or we don't feel close to them, we still cling on to their messages. They play a huge role in the creation of our love myths and messages, and in our love maps. The family is where we first learn about human relationships.

Whatever messages we are fed or pick up on about love in our childhood form our personal attraction factor. We can stay in its grip and be perfectly happy with it, but if we do want to change it we can—it doesn't have to control us. Crucially, the first step is to become aware of what it is. We need to find out who's inside us telling us what to think, how to behave, and what we want. We need to know which parent's message is blueprinting our current relationship or our search for one.

The similarities, threads, and patterns you find being repeated in every relationship don't really have anything to do with the relationship itself—they are all about you. Your choices, your personal magnetism, and your unconscious blueprint and behavior are bringing this to you via the Law of Attraction!

# ESSENTIAL QUESTIONS

When answering the questions below, do so from the perspective of your impression of what happened in your parents' relationship. It's your impression that counts. It doesn't matter whether your brother or sister would agree with you, or if you're not sure that's what your mother would say about herself.

The important insight to gain from this exercise is to see how you perceive your parents, what message they handed down to you, and how their relationship has shaped you.

* What message did your mother give you about love?
* What message did your father give you about love?
* What clues did you pick up from both of them, even if they didn't specifically express them to you?
* Did they conform to the times?
* Did they break the mold?
* Did they follow their hearts?
* Did they "do the right thing"?
* What words would you use to describe their relationship?
* Did your mother grow as a person in the relationship?
* Did your father grow as a person in the relationship?
* Did your mother feel disappointed in the relationship? If so, why?
* Did your father feel disappointed in the relationship? If so, why?
* Did your parents survive tricky times? If so, how?
* What did each of them think about love? (IT'S YOUR IMPRESSION OF THIS THAT COUNTS)
* What did each of them think about marriage?

+ What did each of them think about sex?
+ Do any of the qualities you are attracting or looking for in a partner mirror those of one of your parents? (Be honest here—sometimes we are attracted to qualities that we do not necessarily like, but which repeat something that we have experienced before.)
+ What did your parents hope for you? What did they wish for you?
+ **Now the dynamite question: do you agree with their messages? Think about whether you are living them out, or if there is still a voice inside you that judges potential partners according to your parents" values. Or whether you conduct relationships in a way that mirrors them.**

---

**REVIEW**

Take all this information in. Does it give you insight into what drives you or into the ingredients of your attraction factor?

---

Now we'll look at your own contribution to the mix.

# WHAT IS YOUR LOVE STYLE?

+ How do you approach people?
+ In loving relationships, are you assertive, conciliatory, sensitive, logical, practical, or dynamic?

+ In working relationships, are you assertive, conciliatory, sensitive, logical, practical, or dynamic?
+ If you had to make a choice, would you rather have passion or friendship?
+ Do you like to be independent or dependent?

**REVIEW**

Look at yourself from the outside, or get a friend to explain their perception of you by answering these questions on your behalf.

# IF YOU ARE LOOKING FOR SOMEONE

## WHAT KIND OF PARTNER?

+ What is on your wish list? What is your ideal?
+ What is non-negotiable?
+ What are you open to?
+ What kind of relationship are you looking for: marriage, partnership, friendship?
+ Identify the material specifics you are seeking in a prospective partner:
  [ ] Age, looks, job, income, location
  [ ] Their qualities
  [ ] Their interests
  [ ] Their likes and dislikes
  [ ] Their relationship history

+ And then put down your own material specifics, as if you were joining a dating agency:
  [    ] Your qualities
  [    ] Your interests
  [    ] Your likes and dislikes
  [    ] Your relationship history

## THE DEEPER ISSUES

+ What do you love in life?
+ What are you attracted to? List places, objects, types of people, ideas, vibrations.
+ Are you attracted to difficult people?
+ Are you attracted to people who might be considered emotionally dangerous to you?
+ What do you imagine this partner will do for you? How will they make you feel? What impact will they have on your life?

# IF YOU ARE ALREADY IN A RELATIONSHIP

+ How do you feel in this person's company?
+ Do you feel you present a better version of yourself to other people than you do to your partner? If so, in what ways?
+ What would you change about your partner?
+ What would you change about yourself?

+ What do you want from your partner?
+ What do they give you?
+ What do they not give you?
+ Why do you want this person in your life?
+ What do you consider to be your main problem or issue in the relationship?
+ What would be your wish for, or what would you want to attract to the relationship?

## YOUR RELATIONSHIP HISTORY

**Make a list of your significant relationships. This is not to determine the amount of time they lasted, but to reveal the impact they had on you.**

List how each one started, and how it made you feel, and if this feeling changed, why it did. List what you expected out of each relationship, how it ended, and what you got out of it in terms of life lessons and experience. And indicate whether you still feel you have unfinished business with this person. If you do, then move to the section on "Letting Go of Past Relationships" (see page 115).

# WHEN TO BE SPECIFIC AND WHEN TO GO WITH THE FLOW: THE CONTRADICTION THAT IS LIFE'S MYSTERY

If you are looking for a new relationship, it's helpful to be very clear about the kind of person you want in your life.

You can, of course, write down a wish list. For example, six foot, with a six-pack, Brad Pitt lookalike, thirty to thirty-five years old, rich, unattached, successful, and so on. But remember that the Law of Attraction will not necessarily send you exactly what you want.

Take the joke about the husband and wife, both sixty years old, whose fairy godmother told them they would each be allowed one wish. The wife asked to be sent on a cruise around the world with her darling husband, and it was granted. Then it was her husband's turn, and he asked for a woman thirty years younger than him. The fairy godmother waved her magic wand and suddenly the husband was sitting on the deck of a cruise liner, ninety years old, with his sixty-year-old wife beside him!

It's good to be specific, if only to clear out any resistance or confusion in your own head. Sometimes it's helpful to imagine yourself living out an exact desire or intention. You see it becoming real, and in some cases, you'll immediately realize that your "perfect" plan has flaws, that you may in fact not want to be with the person you idealized, or it might bring up other issues. The saying, "be careful what you wish for" is very appropriate. You have to make sure you are ready, willing, and able to live with the outcome of a dream come true.

# INTERNET DATING
# AND SPEED DATING

Dating agencies or internet matchmaking sites tend to focus on the visible world rather than the invisible one. This means your key patterns, hooks, and secret agenda will go unnoticed—that is until they surface on a date. Internet dating in particular has a virtual-reality quality. It can reduce people to commodities, like books or CDs. This automatically puts your mind and energy in a different dating zone. If you download somebody from the internet, and put them in your shopping cart, then you won't be able to pick up on their energy in the same way you would if you had met him or her in real life.

In some cases people meet up and are very happy with their internet date and end up getting married. The internet can also get you going, if you're a receptive rather than a dynamic type and you need to start the ball rolling. But it pays to be aware that by its very nature the internet creates a different vibrational energy that can interfere with our highly sensitive intuitive radar.

At least speed dating gives you the chance to see the person and pick tip on whether you have an energy match. As in the world "out there," it could be argued that people tend to reveal themselves in the first five minutes. It is said that if you go for an interview or view a property, the key decision is made in the first five minutes, even though you might spend half an hour discussing job prospects or plumbing systems.

So, speed dating may be onto something. Perhaps everything we need to know about someone is there in the first five minutes we share with them before they move on to someone else. In those few moments we might be more acutely aware of what they say, how they sound, and how we feel in their presence than we would if we had spent a couple of hours with them. Speed dating really gets your energy and your listening gear working acutely. But even if you're not speed dating you should view everyone you meet as if you were. Because if you have all your antennae switched on, you will see that everybody reveals a lot about themselves without realizing it. What are they choosing to talk about? What are they conveying with their body language? And how do they make you feel?

**Don't forget you've already got the most powerful and effective dating agency in the world already at your fingertips—it's called the Law of Attraction! And it's absolutely free.**

# CHAPTER 4

# What's Your Type?

## RELATIONSHIP TYPES— WHAT WE DRAW TO US

We can use the Law of Attraction to help bring a special someone into our lives. Alternatively, we can use it to break out of a relationship pattern. The magnetism of this law of resonance allows us only to attract those people that mirror our inner self. Outwardly, we may say we're looking for X, but we keep getting Y, and we can't understand why we're yet again with a commitment-phobe or a control freak.

How does it happen? For starters, we're bombarded with the available, visible information about a person, which makes it harder to spot the psychological patterns that we are magnetizing. Yet, if we look at our pattern, identify it, and realize where it comes from and what it's all about, then we can start thinking different thoughts and making new choices that will break the pattern.

Don't forget: The pattern originates with us. We are doing something to attract this type of person—giving out a particular message or inwardly believing something about ourselves that goes out into the cosmos like a heat-seeking missile. We are giving out our expectations to the universe all the time without even realizing it. The trick is to become conscious of what we're thinking.

Thoughts are going around in our heads all the time—when we're traveling to work, at the gym, preparing a meal, or in front of the TV. Often they are "mindless" thoughts, but whatever it is we're thinking about—certain people, specific situations—then that's what we're attracting. You've heard the expression used when suddenly someone wakes up to the fact that he or she's made a mistake—"What was I thinking?" **It pays to be aware of what you're thinking at all times.** But even if you're waking up to some mistake of your own, the beauty of the Law of Attraction is that you can shift what's going on by changing how you think.

We know quite confidently when someone is "not our type," which is when they don't meet our standards. Yet it's our inner psychological standards that need to be explored. Our types and patterns act as magnets at all times, ironically, for the exact opposite of what we consciously want. That's when we get the oil-and-vinegar couples, who nevertheless "go together," and the giver-and-taker and parent-and-child types, who are busy dovetailing their roles—equally feeding off and needing one another. The committed type and the free spirit are pulling in opposite directions and are generating a magnetic attraction between each other.

Here are some of the relationship types that keep us in a specific familiar pattern. There's nothing wrong with being in that pattern if you're happy with it. But if you recognize yourself and your relationship in any of these scenarios and you would like to break free of the cycle, then you need to do something about it. Awareness makes a huge difference when it comes to attracting what you want. Once you've truly "gotten" what's happening inside you in terms of your patterns, and have become aware of what you really want, then you can change everything with the power of your intention.

# GIVER AND TAKER

## THE GIVER

The giver is the one who constantly accommodates the other person. You know that you're one if you're prepared to drop everything at the last minute in order to fit in with someone else's plans.

Givers turn up on time. They automatically think it's their job to pick up the bathroom towels, make the beds, and arrive home with fresh bread for the next day. Givers always remember anniversaries, buy presents, write thank you notes, and generally make an effort to please. They are people-pleasers. But it is not that they are entirely selfless, because they get their kicks out of giving to others. In extreme cases they feel martyred, which also lends them a perverse feel-good factor. They are compelled to be the "good person." It is difficult to have an equal relationship with a compulsive giver, because the other person always feels he or she is in debt. In some cases giving can have a secret control factor.

### The Payoff

It's great to be the "good one" in a relationship. You occupy the moral high ground, and so your partner's faults appear magnified in contrast.

### What is the Pattern?

Givers are generally born into families where their own needs are not met. Hence the desire to meet other people's needs in order to replay the psychological pattern. Even though givers get the payoff of feeling saintly, they are frequently left with the familiar feeling that their own needs have not been met. The pattern is then confirmed. They tend to attract takers because of their own need to be needed.

**HOW TO IDENTIFY A GIVER**

+ Always available to take a phone call
+ Avoids conflict
+ A good listener
+ Lets the other person go first
+ Lets the other person do the choosing
+ Tries to smooth the life and path of the other person

## THE TAKER

Takers possess a strong sense of entitlement. Their under-lying belief is that the world and everybody in it owes them. Takers are happy to let other people pick up after them, to lie in bed while someone else makes the coffee, and to use up all the hot water for themselves. They don't remember to pass messages on to others. At the worst extreme, takers aren't even interested enough in others to ask them anything about their lives.

Conversations with takers revolve around them, and they tend to dominate the atmosphere with their opinions and moods. Everybody else is there as a backdrop to their own starring role. It never occurs to them that others might be tired, bored, hungry, or have something else they want to talk about, because other people are viewed as mere satellites of the taker's all-absorbing world.

Of course takers don't verbalize this, but their psycho-logical blueprint is narcissistic. Any arrangement is made to suit them. When a taker wants to see you, they first state their own availability and preferred venue, with an innate assumption that you will fit in with them.

### The Payoff

It goes without saying: Takers' needs are usually met; they do what they want to do. They have a relationship on their own terms.

### What is the Pattern?

The taker's mentality might develop from an only-child syndrome, where the child is the center of attention and cannot ever bear to grow up. But takers can just as easily be born into larger families, where they coerce their siblings into doing what they want.

People often give in to them, because takers tend to be bullies or create such a fuss that others decide it simply isn't worth standing up to them. In fact, takers are often insecure, and deep down they do not possess a strong sense of their own center. They only feel alive when others are showing them attention. They frequently attract givers.

**HOW TO IDENTIFY A TAKER**

+ A "me first" attitude
+ Talks constantly about him or herself
+ Doesn't appreciate what is given
+ Makes assumptions about the other person
+ Has high expectations of the other person

# VARIATIONS ON GIVER AND TAKER

## LEADER AND FOLLOWER

In the leader-and-follower relationship one person sets the pace and makes most of the decisions, while the other is prepared to give up their job or move home to be together.

The follower is always playing catch-up, because the leader constantly takes off in different new directions.

## LOVER AND BELOVED

There is always a theme of pursuit here, with the lover firing arrows of desire at the beloved. The one that is loved keeps up a game of mystery, which ensures the lover is kept interested. This type of game intrigues those who like a challenge, while being an object of desire is flattering for the ego.

# THE COMMITTED AND THE FREE SPIRIT

## THE COMMITTED

The committed type has a great need to settle down, feel secure, and know where they stand. They are inherently loyal, never looking over your shoulder to see if someone more interesting has walked into the room. They see relationships as unfolding in progressive stages and culminating in marriage. The committed type is prepared to take on everything, including your family and any children from a previous relationship. They take on excess baggage. It goes without saying that the committed type is in the relationship for the long haul. They plan for years ahead and like to develop rituals within the relationship, which they see as cementing the bond.

## The Payoff

The committed type gets to know where they stand with someone by forming a structure around the relationship. They thrive on steadiness.

## What is the Pattern?

Committed types fall into two categories. One originates from a family in which the parents are glued together and the pattern is what psychologists would call "meshed." In other words, the family is interdependent and functions as a complete entity. So, any new relationship is expected to fit into the larger family as a whole. However, the other category of the committed type comes from exactly the opposite scenario. Their family origin has disintegrated as a unit, and so they are determined to put their personal lives back together again in the form of a solid relationship. Either way, committed types are looking for someone else to commit to them to fulfill their own dream of stability.

---

### HOW TO IDENTIFY A COMMITTED TYPE

+ Talks about the relationship in positive terms
+ Sees the relationship as occupying a central place in the wider context of their life
+ Is available for the other person
+ Isn't afraid to talk about the future
+ Doesn't indulge in playing games to keep the other person dangling

---

# THE FREE SPIRIT

Free spirits are a law unto themselves when it comes to relationships. They are usually attracted to a wide variety of people, rather than having "a type." Free spirits see no problem in running relationships concurrently because they feel that no one owns them. They defy possession and justify their non-committal attitude as being an intelligent, post-modern response. They are most likely to say that they don't need a piece of paper in order to "feel married."

Free spirits resist convention, and are always in the process of seeing how a relationship goes rather than steering it toward a greater commitment. A fear of intimacy means that this type frequently avoids spending time just in the couple, and feels more comfortable when the primary relationship is diluted by the company of others.

## The Payoff

Free spirits keep their options open, which gives them a wider pool of people to draw upon. They are unhindered by conventional ties—and even if they are in a relationship, they still remain free spirits.

## What is the Pattern?

Free spirits tend to be serial daters. They can't take a relationship beyond the initial excitement stage, because once the lust and sparkle die down they are terrified of being trapped in boredom.

Commitment-phobes are often created from damage in childhood. On the surface, the family may seem very close. But often one of the parents has lionized the child and made him or her into a little prince or princess. In this case, the free-spirit personality type has been so smothered by a parent that deep down they feel they cannot be unfaithful to Mommy or Daddy.

Some free spirits come from an unconventional family, where previous generations defied convention in the settling-down stakes. Or they might have their own reasons for not wishing to repeat family patterns, and therefore protect themselves by running free.

---

**HOW TO IDENTIFY A FREE SPIRIT**

+ Always talks about "I" instead of "We"
+ Makes arrangements to do things independently, without involving the other person
+ Disappears at parties and gives the impression they are available, even if they are already in a relationship
+ Has a restless, highly sociable personality and likes to act spontaneously
+ Dislikes routine and gets bored easily

---

# PARENT AND CHILD

## THE PARENT

The parent type frequently adopts a slightly scolding, patronizing attitude toward their partner which implies that they know it all. They often earn significantly more than their partner and therefore cast themselves in the role of the person doling out the goodies. The parent is the controller, who thinks they know best. Parental types often lay down the rules of the relationship and make all the running.

## The Payoff

The parent feels secure when they are in control. The imbalance in the relationship makes them feet superior.

## What is the Pattern?

Often the parent type is an eldest child who is used to bossing around their siblings, or even playing parent to them. Parent types are often given responsibility from a young age and feel old beyond their years. They have a need to look after another person, but not in the same way as the giver—because the unspoken message is that the giving is strictly on the parent's terms and not on the recipient's. Sometimes the parent type is trying to redress the balance of a chaotic childhood, where they felt their parents did not look after them enough. By creating this strong and powerful role for themselves they hope to ensure that they will never feel helpless or vulnerable.

---

**HOW TO IDENTIFY A PARENT TYPE**

+ Feels happiest paying for themselves and others

+ Opinionated and fixed in their ideas

+ Organizes and manages holidays, social events, house purchasing

+ Offers unsolicited advice

+ Attached to their position or role in the world

+ Takes on responsibilities

---

# THE CHILD

The child type doesn't want to grow up or take on responsibility in life. They see themselves as young, developing individuals, somewhat fragile and incapable of earning a decent living. They tend to get carried away with plans and dreams of the future, which often turn out to be impractical, or they lose interest in them. The child type is needy. They want others to help, support, and inform them, and never to do anything for themselves if someone else can do it for them.

The child types tend to get away with things because they project an image of vulnerability. Deep down they believe they are too special to have to deal with the ordinary mundane things of the grown-up world. They could never do a job that was "boring," or be in a relationship that required "hard work."

## The Payoff

The adult "child" is often strangely attractive—particularly to the parent type, who wants to take care of them. The child is paid for, taken to places and indulged.

## What is the Pattern?

Child types often come from families who never encouraged their children to grow up. Perhaps the mother smothered the child, who then played into the mother's need to be needed. When searching for a relationship the child types are unconsciously looking for a mother or father figure to replicate their early life. The child types often encourage someone else to look after them by asking for advice or help, laying out their problems, or saying they are "hopeless with money." They present themselves as either a damsel in distress, a creative, head-in-the-clouds person, or someone "hard done by" in their relationships. They then lure their knight in shining armor or their sugar mama in to their nursery world.

---

**HOW TO IDENTIFY A CHILD TYPE**

+ Happy to be paid for

+ Doesn't know what they want to do

+ Appears to need help/advice/support

+ Lets others take control and make arrangements for them

+ Doesn't have any plans for the future beyond being taken care of

---

# THE TWO HALVES RELATIONSHIP

This kind of relationship is characterized by two people that see one another as equals, regardless of their position, income, age, or experience. They are able to switch roles according to whatever is most needed at the time, because they see themselves primarily as a unit in which the good of the relationship takes precedence over their individual preferences. Although they function as two halves of a whole, each one is also perfectly able to operate as an individual in his or her own right.

# CHAPTER 5

# Patterns and Blocks
## How We Prevent Our Desires from Being Fulfilled

## THE DENIAL AND DEFENSES AROUND YOUR HEART

### THE "I NEVER MEET ANYONE" TYPE

Extraordinarily, given the over six billion people milling around in the world, one of the most common phrases spoken by people who are looking for a relationship is that they "never meet anybody." What is really happening here? Usually these people lead busy lives, hold down jobs that put them in contact with hundreds of people, have access to the internet, travel, and possess huge numbers of friends.

The person who says they never meet anyone really means they are not meeting "the one." Actually they are coming across lots of people—but none that are deemed "suitable." They may be shielding themselves from the possibility of a relationship, but denying that they are doing this. They could be cutting themselves off from opportunities of meeting the kind of person with whom they could form a happy alliance, without consciously realizing that they are doing it.

The joke about defense mechanisms is that no one thinks they've got them. They operate in secret, so we don't even realize they are there. They have a good and important job to do, but they also tend to get in the way, like bouncers at a nightclub. Obviously, we need defenses to ensure our physical safety. But when it comes to our emotional lives we need to defend ourselves from anxiety. Breaking the mold and going for a big change (such as getting involved in a new relationship) can be stressful. So, not much wonder that it's far easier to keep the protective shutters down and pretend it's nothing to do with us, but that we just don't meet the right people.

However, defenses need to be handled with care. They are not to be ripped away, leaving us vulnerable and exposed. We need to go gently and realize that defenses serve a purpose—they keep us going. Without them we imagine we will fall to pieces or our lives will be thrust into highly uncomfortable change. Of course, all this goes on inside our heads automatically. We do not consciously know we are defended. It is our invisible "keep out" sign.

When I hear someone say, "I never meet anybody," I envision the person actually wearing the phrase, like a suit of armor. It is one of the best defenses going. Usually there is an undercurrent of irritation accompanying the phrase, because the person often truly believes they are actively seeking a relationship. What I hear underneath the surface is, "I am stuck and blocked in my quest for a soulmate, and I'm giving up and feeling hopeless about it. It's not me, it's them." (Whoever "they" might be, because I haven't met them!) The unspoken belief is that the soul mate is deliberately hiding from this person, evading them, despite his or her best efforts—which is why they feel angry and frustrated about it.

"I never meet anybody" is a full-stop phrase. It's a bleak statement of fact. A negative meditation. Imagine how the universe hears it! There is no light or optimism accompanying this thought. There is no possibility of change and no room to meet anyone. It is a mantra that is self-fulfilling.

The "I never meet anybody" type will often have an answer for every stone that has been left unturned. The more suggestions that are made as to what steps they could take, the more the note of defiance creeps into their voice. "I have tried that," they might exclaim, or give some other reason why they can't make the salsa class, or say they believe that someone younger than them would never be interested. Even if they hear about amazing relationships happening to other people they quickly say, "That would never happen to me." Holding this self-limiting belief will ensure no opportunities for love will slip through their tightly bound world.

Scratch the surface of the "not meeting anybody" type and you will quickly see that they are hugely invested in things remaining the same. Staying in the groove. Although, of course, this is buried so deep that if someone dared to point it out they would be hurt, defensive, and angry.

The more these difficult feelings churn around inside somebody, the more they leak out on the surface. You might believe that you are open to meeting somebody and are just waiting to find Mr. or Miss Right. And you might go through the motions of turning up at events, making an effort to look good, and chatting to people, but the "I never meet anybody" part of you is actually running the show. You need to replace this mantra with a more positive one.

In order to move on, the part of you that doesn't want to break the pattern needs to be neutralized. Awareness of the power you have to change your situation is everything—you need to be clear about what you want to do.

You can start by listening to yourself saying that you never meet anybody—catch yourself doing it. That's the first step toward reprogramming yourself. The resigned air that accompanies the statement speaks of a long, deeply ingrained problem. "I never meet anybody" is an angry but wistful longing for contact, a fear of rejection, and a belief that the world/universe is a difficult place that doesn't meet your needs. That the person ("my Mr./Miss Right") is withholding him or herself from you—and that's before you've even met! The phrase speaks volumes about your pattern. Everything is contained within it. Your impatience, frustration, and fear is present in the room as you confide in a friend, who feels the tension as you speak. It can prompt a reaction in them—the urge to make it better—which, inevitably, is met with a rebuff.

The "I never meet anybody" type thinks of the universe as a withholding parent, and of themselves as the child, powerless to alter the status quo. At the same time they wonder what they are doing wrong. They might be making a great effort to do all the right things, but their own inner image and perception of themselves as a child in the face of an unfair, controlling, denying universe is blocking anything new from happening.

## SAYING IT BUT NOT BELIEVING IT

You need to become aware of your own resistance. For those who say, "I want to meet someone," ask why it doesn't happen. Ask yourself what is stopping or preventing it. Start living as if you already have someone in your life—by making your living arrangements couple friendly for instance, then you're actively fast tracking your attraction factor.

## YOUR HIDDEN AGENDA

You might believe yourself to be an open person, simply wanting to meet someone. However, although you say "someone," it's not just anyone. It's Mr. or Miss Right, who looks like X, earns Y, and has the qualities of Z. It's always the specifics that stand in the way. If you are looking for your dream partner, that is precisely what it will remain—a dream. You need to look for your real partner.

Unconsciously, some people are looking for a powerful, wealthy partner who they believe will take away their insecurity. For instance, they are only attracted to alpha males and, even though they may have had some disappointing experiences with them, this remains their unconscious blueprint. There is nothing wrong with seeking a highly successful mate. However, because success is what drives the alpha male, he often has less quality time to give to other areas, which means he is often emotionally unavailable.

You might come from a family where your parents have such a wonderful marriage that it's a hard act to follow. On the other hand, you might only be attracted to those who let you down or fail to commit, because it mirrors something in your parents' relationship.

---

Being aware of your own hidden agenda is key. Realizing that you have concealed expectations and that these are keeping you stuck is a crucial component of what will make the Law of Attraction for Love work for you.

---

Is it an unfair world out there? Yes. We don't always get what we want. But we also have a part to play in creating the unfairness and in generating our own patterns. Our resistance comes through because something within us is saying, "No, this is too scary." You are creating your own impasse. You think you can't do something, or you're actually stopping it from happening. You are caught in a strange bind, where the more you want it, the more the counterforce comes in.

# SO YOU WANT A RELATIONSHIP— IS RESISTANCE STOPPING YOU?

## WHAT IS RESISTANCE?

It is whatever stops or blocks us from within. Resistance reveals a fear of letting ourselves go into the unknown.

*How do you know when it's operating?* Whenever you feel powerless or stuck—this is a great clue that resistance is going on. When you have a problem, there is usually an equal part of yourself that doesn't want to find the solution.

*What are the other symptoms of resistance?* Feeling blank about what you can do or confused as to what your next step should be. The mental fog is something you create so that you don't have to make a decision. You can't read the signals the universe is trying to send you unless you're aware and awake.

*Why do we stay stuck?* There is usually a hidden payoff in remaining stuck. It feels safer to stay where you are, even though you want the change. Resistance performs an important role in looking after us. It shuts out difficult problems and protects us from the very things that scare us. If we talk about wanting a relationship, but have a fear of intimacy deep down, then resistance will pop up and keep us away from the perceived threat. It's a really invisible business and you have to be prepared to be very honest with yourself in order to see it. Hardly anyone will actually own up to a fear of intimacy. We can't even admit it to ourselves. If we don't want to see, acknowledge, or look at it then it will go under the surface and become the biggest block to our ability to meet someone.

The natural instinct might be to fight the resistance. To try to cut it out, remove it in one fell swoop. But that would expose us too much. It is not as simple as that, and we need to acknowledge our need for protection. The first step is actually to embrace the resistance: to know why it's there. To realize that it's useful in some ways, but at the same time is keeping us stuck. We can't just say, "Now I will simply stop being resistant."

We have to see how it comes into play, what kind of situations make it active. To see where our buttons are being pressed, and how resistance rushes in to defend us from danger. We may be yearning for a relationship but it is simply too dangerous for us to enter into that emotional, intimate territory.

We stay stuck with our old lives if we don't make room for something new to happen. The minute you **expect** things to be different then you will start attracting something different.

# DEFENSES

## THE STORIES WE TELL OURSELVES

The more fragile we are, the more defenses we need, because the world doesn't feel safe to us. We carry around this emotional insurance policy, but it costs a lot. In fact, it takes a lot out of us to keep it going. We have to keep investing in our defense patterns, to keep feeding ourselves the same story.

Nicki had already gone through a painful divorce and threw herself into an active social life but constantly told me "There are no men out there"—this was her denial and her defense; it became *her* truth, even though it was not the truth and it didn't reflect her true hopes. I asked her, "What would happen if there were?"

At the same time you are telling yourself (and anyone else who will listen) the same story over and over again, you are running another possible storyline which you also tell yourself and the world—that you really want to meet somebody. It is energy fighting energy. You are doing this to yourself. You long for something and then resist it, don't believe in it, run away from it, or sabotage it.

Some of the stories we tell ourselves are guaranteed to keep us narrow and limited. We can call these "rackets." We keep the racket going and we kid ourselves that the reason we can't do X, Y, or Z is because we don't have the money, the time, or the opportunity. We are being dishonest with ourselves, and this boils down to our own fear of change. We won't take the risk.

We all tend to occupy familiar territory in life. We go to the same places, do the same things, hang out with the same people—and we inhabit the same emotional territory too. It feels safe; we know what to expect. And we cut ourselves off from letting anything new happen. In ancient times the world was believed to be square, with definite edges that were dangerous. Legend has it that maps were once drawn with "here be dragons" written in the outside margin, indicating the unknown. Of course, we now know the world is round and that we won't fall over the edge, but we still create our own imaginary boundaries, or edges, where we simply won't go—either physically or psychologically.

We can become so invested in the myth of who we are that we close ourselves off to our potential. We form identities around the job we do, how old we are and what we've got—and they become set in stone. The more we believe in these superficial indications of who we are, the less likely we are to feel truly free. It becomes more difficult to act spontaneously; we turn down invitations because we think we won't enjoy the experience. We become denser in our thinking patterns and more emotionally blocked as we remain fixated in these roles, identities, and expectations. We expend all of our energy in holding on to what we've got and who we are. But the truth is that we could reinvent ourselves if we wanted to. We always have a choice, and yet it's so easy to forget this.

# HOW MUCH FREEDOM DO WE REALLY HAVE?

The answer to this question, within the free world, is as much as you want or as much as you think you have. We actually live in a void that we fill by creating our own personal comfort zones. And once we have stepped into our comfort zone, life continues to send us our delivery every week and we don't think to change it. So many things are pulled in toward us by our existing patterns and mindset. We attract them in, and then wonder why we always end up with the same things! Come back to the present and be aware of what you're thinking right this minute. Keep bringing yourself back to your intention all through the day. Make it your mental screen saver, so it's always there, reminding you to focus on what you want, not what you don't want. The power to turn your life around rests with your own ability to be aware of what you're thinking.

The power of the Law of Attraction is so enormous that you will realize it's a no-brainer to stop closing yourself down, and open yourself up to possibilities.

# QUESTIONS TO ASK YOURSELF ABOUT YOUR STORY

+ What is my story/my pattern around relationships?
+ How did it come into being? Think about your childhood story, your parents' relationship.
+ How do I keep myself stuck and blocked?
+ How would I like things to be?
+ Am I willing to rewrite the script?
+ Write down anything relevant—any insight into your story.

# CHAPTER 6

# The Hard-Work Miracle

## HOW TO MAKE THE LAW OF ATTRACTION WORK FOR YOU ...

So, now you are aware of your wish list. In theory, you know what you want. And you've looked at some of the things that might be standing in the way, such as defenses, patterns and your story.

Now it's time to go one step further. This chapter will give you specific techniques to work through anything that might be preventing your desires from manifesting. You will be working on yourself here: questioning, analyzing, visualizing, and meditating.

The Law of Attraction is a combination of miracles and hard work!

Getting closer to your dream happens in little moments, through small choices—we need to dare to be different. Sometimes a slight change can make a really big impression and be very encouraging.

However, we shouldn't expect to shift a huge pattern of resistance overnight. The universe can't deliver what you want through a heavy field of defense or denial. It just isn't possible. You need to clear your energy field so that the universe can fulfill your desires.

That means doing some work on yourself: some assessment and appraisal. If you don't feel able to answer the questions below by yourself, then get someone you trust to answer them on your behalf. This can be a very interesting exercise, as the other person will often be able to see straight through your defenses and into the heart of the matter.

Do some visualizations and meditations, and then activate your will by taking your next step. Keep going. Stay motivated. Don't give up on yourself—or on the universe.

# EVEN IF NOTHING'S EVER WORKED SO FAR

Your next step is to focus on where you are stuck and how to change your position.

**Remember, You are the One Who Creates Your Reality**

Here are some questions to ask yourself:

+ What is it that I really want?
+ Why do I want it?

+ What is stopping me from having it?

    a) The universe isn't delivering

    b) I'm not sure if it's possible

    c) I'm trying everything, but nothing happens

    d) I'm afraid that if I had it I wouldn't be up to it

    e) I'm worried about change or the unknown

    f) I am protecting myself

    g) I don't know (which is your resistance in operation)

    h) Another reason

+ What is my payoff in remaining stuck, in not having this desire delivered? Am I getting anything out of life by staying the same?

+ What would my life look like and how would I feel if I carried on like this forever?

+ Do I have times when I feel I'm moving forward? If so, when? In what circumstances? What happens to block it again?

+ How did I get into this situation? List events, attitudes and people that have contributed to this present problem. What did they do? What did I do?

+ Do I believe it is possible for the situation to change?

+ Is it possible for me to change?

---

Visualize your block as a brick that is made up of all the insights you have gleaned from your response to these questions. Now lay it down as the foundation stone of your powerful intention to make the Law of Attraction work for you. You will build up from here.

# TECHNIQUES TO KEEP YOUR ENERGY FLOWING

Now you need some techniques, in case you become stuck, to get the energy moving again so you can start to make things happen. Remember, you may not be able to enforce a change, but you can free up the energy and get it moving again.

Being able to attract what it is you desire requires you to work on your ability to pull things toward you. Being able to manifest what you want on the physical plane is an art which can be perfected. In order to pull things out of the air, you need to develop greater magnetism.

First, you need to state your intentions in whatever way you wish.

1. *Write down your wishes and send them out to the powers that be.* Put them on your fridge where you constantly see them.

2. *Ask yourself what the next three steps would be to get things moving for you.* Write them down. Make them achievable, manageable, and possible within a short time frame.

3. *Tell a mentor* what you're about to do and get him or her to check in with you to see if you're still on the case.

4. *Acting as if ... the realistic fantasy.* Now imagine that you are living life without this problem. Or that your wish has already been fulfilled. You radiate out a feeling of having it now. If it's hard to imagine then ask yourself:

+ If you were free of your problem what would *your life* be like?
+ If you were free of your problem what would *you* be like?
+ How would you act and how would you be?
+ Get in touch with how you would feel if your intention had already manifested. Amplify this emotion, feel it in your body, in your mind, and in all of your being. To be able to experience this, to imagine having your desire and living it out, is really important.
+ When you've gotten hold of this feeling, write down any words that describe it. What is it? Do you know anyone else who lives like this or who embodies this feeling? Could you try to embody it yourself?

Your mission now is to act as if this fantasy has already become reality. Act as if you are already living out your desires—you are it, you have it. Even if what you wanted to happen hasn't happened, just act as if it has. Whenever and wherever you can. If you create a separation between yourself and your wish then it becomes harder for it to manifest. You must *be* whatever your wish is, connect with it, become it, or act as if you are aligning yourself with it. Seeing your wish as obtainable is a crucial factor in getting it delivered.

This technique subtly alters your attraction pattern. It works on the premise that "like attracts like" and you become able to magnetize the people and situations that you want in your life.

Another effective technique to increase your power of pulling things toward you and to give you more leverage in life is "the magnet meditation." This great little exercise can be used to build up your resources of self-esteem and make you feel more positive and confident about getting what you want—any time, any place, anywhere.

5. *The magnet meditation.* Imagine you are a magnet. Picture yourself as being infused with magnetic energy that attracts whatever you want. Imagine your desires coming toward you simply because they are being pulled in your direction. Become aware of how easily life works when you have this magnetic energy. How simple it is to get what you want. But there is a caveat: Be careful what you wish for. The magnet meditation is very powerful and you need to know that you're attracting the right things rather than all kinds of stuff that you thought you wanted but is really just excess baggage.

If you are still wrestling with issues that are bringing you down, then try the following higher-perspective meditation.

## GAINING A HIGHER PERSPECTIVE ON THE PROBLEM

Find somewhere comfortable and quiet, where you won't be interrupted, and sit with your back straight. Close your eyes and breathe deeply. Let go of any tension in your body and feel it leaving you.

Now visualize yourself sitting as you are on the chair. Mentally look down on yourself sitting in the room and become aware that you are meditating on a particular issue in your life. See the room vividly in your mind, with its furniture and colors. Imagine looking down on the house or building from above, with you inside it. Now imagine you are seeing this scene from even higher up; you can see the street, the town, and everyone going about their day-to-day business, while you are sitting inside on a chair, in a room, in your house. Now go higher still and see the country you are living in, and see the whole world with all its countries and people. Send positive energy from this position down to yourself, as if you are sitting under a spotlight.

Visualize yourself with this problem and run through the patterns and events that have led up to it, as if rewinding a film. Only the relevant parts will be shown to you. Is there a thread you can see? Is there anything you can see from up here that you didn't know about down there? Are there any words, inspirations, feelings, or advice you can send down to yourself from your higher point of awareness?

Slowly come back down to earth, become aware of the world, your own country, your own town, your own street, your own house, the room you are in, the chair you are sitting on. Wiggle your toes and hands, open your eyes, and come back. Write down what you have experienced, how you felt, and any help you may have gained.

If you find it difficult to believe and trust that your wish will be granted, or you find it hard to stop trying to control everything, then try the following technique.

## TECHNIQUE FOR GOING WITH THE FLOW

Allow yourself to drop into a meditative, contemplative state. Feel the relaxation in your body where all effort has dropped away. Imagine you are looking at a river that will take you where you want to go—all you have to do is to get in (this is safe water, not rapids) and float along, allowing its gentle current to carry you to your final destination. The river may meander, but that's fine. You have enough time. You don't need to worry about the journey, or steer, or make anything happen. Flow along with the river. Experience what it feels like to place your trust in something else. Let go of any desire to control—just watch the scenery, enjoy the experience, and know that you will arrive at a place that is right for you.

This technique is useful to repeat whenever you are getting stressed about the whys, hows, and wherefores of life. If you can't get a handle on what to do next, try the following technique.

## THE CHOICE MEDITATION

Imagine you are walking along the path of your life. Then you come to a fork in the road. You have to make a choice. Imagine you have a map and can see where each road leads. Look at what the map is telling you about these two choices. Is one a faster route than the other? Is one more beautiful? Will one get you to your destination in a far simpler way? Will the other involve the possibility of getting lost? Do both roads lead to the same place, so whichever one you take will be okay? Or are you about to go in a very different direction? Realize that you are free to move whichever way you want in your journey through life.

All of these exercises and techniques will help you increase your *power of attainment.* But there is one ingredient that is essential to your skill in manifesting what you want. It is the power of intention.

# WHAT IS THE DIFFERENCE BETWEEN INTENTION AND DESIRE?

We need to turn up the volume of intention if the law of attraction is to work for us. Having an intention is very different to having a desire, and if you want the law of attraction to manifest your deepest wishes, then intention is everything.

What exactly is *intention* as opposed to *desire?* Intention is a conscious state. It implies purpose, taking responsibility for what happens, and being 100% behind getting something done. For example, if you intend to lose weight, then it's likely you will go on a diet, do more exercise, set goals, and do everything in your power to break bad habits. Desire, on the other hand, is defined as "an unsatisfied longing." It is a passive state. So if you only desire to lose weight, you may want to drop some pounds or wish it would happen, but it's not going to unless you do something about it.

**If we come from a place of intention then things start to pull together.** They become connected. However, if we come from a place of desire then we experience fragmentation, where all our desires are competing with one another. We can get lost in this realm; sometimes our desires are in so much conflict with each other that we lose sight of what it is that we really want. If we are driven by our desires they can be so powerful that they feel compulsive. And the unfortunate thing is that even if we do fulfill them, they are rarely satisfying for long. Once we have achieved one desire then we are pulled toward having more of it, or to reaching out for the next one. Whatever it was we wanted, when we eventually get it we realize that it still isn't enough for us. We're in a cycle that keeps us on a hamster wheel.

It may seem as if desire makes the world go round. Corporations thrive on it; advertising promotes it; and we chase around after this or that, thinking it will make us happy. Yet when our energy is scattered we are less effective. In the pursuit of desire we sometimes waste our essence, our substance, our vital life force. It's important not to identify with desires too much—they are what carry us away, often into old habits.

But feeling desire is not all bad. It can be a positive thing, because desire puts us in touch with what we want. It can be the trigger to shake us out of our inertia. It can be good to desire something and to want an outcome, but it's best not to get too attached or stuck in a mindset about how it can be delivered. By its very nature attachment is intense. When we're totally attached to having what we want then we feel our lives depend upon it.

According to Buddhist theory, desire and attachment are major sources of unhappiness. The Dalai Lama talks of "a non-needful beingness," which doesn't grasp or cling either to objects, situations, or people. You might think that using the Law of Attraction goes against this principle, because it implies that we want something. We do. But the real secret of working with the Law of Attraction hinges on our ability to intend something to happen, without feeling compulsive about it.

You can avoid compulsive attachment by cultivating intention. Intention is more purposeful and mindful than desire. With intention you can experience maximum energy with minimum effort.

Using intention means you are operating from a greater level of self-awareness. You *choose to do something, rather than have to. By* using intention you can meet your needs rather than your wants.

# DO YOU MAKE YOUR OWN LUCK?

**THINK LUCKY!**

Research has shown that if you think of yourself as lucky then you attract more opportunities.

It all sounds so easy, as if you can get everything you want simply by asking for it, and that all you need to do is lie back and wait for it to come knocking on your door. But I don't believe it really works like that. Particularly if you have any patterns of resistance that will make it harder for new possibilities to come through.

## KEY WAYS TO GET LUCKY

This is how you make your own luck and, as someone once said, "I had to work very hard to get this lucky!"

+ It's not enough just to *want* something to happen, you have to be prepared to do something about it too. The universe expects you to do your part. Making an effort is also a key ingredient. You attract opportunities by knowing how to use them, just as energy follows energy. You will need to start developing the attitude and the intention to make clear choices and firm decisions to head in a chosen direction.

+ If you've been trying everything, but feel as though you're knocking your head against a brick wall, you might need to **trust the process** more so that the Law of Attraction can work for you. It's not about being in control and having everything you want, but about trusting and letting go, so that the universe can get through and deliver. You might need to develop a willingness to surrender to a flow of energy that will get you where you want to go.

+ But here is the paradox behind creating luck: be 100% behind it, but do not allow yourself to get attached to the outcome. And don't get attached to how it has to happen. The minute you start boxing yourself in with elaborate detail about how you want things to be, then the delivery system gets blocked. The technique of being committed to an event happening, without trying to control it, requires some patience and practice. But once you've got it, luck will follow.

# ARE YOU A RECEPTIVE OR DYNAMIC ENERGY TYPE?

This brings us back to the theme of fate or free will. To what extent can we affect the outcome? People tend to fall into two types: the more receptive type feels that there is a larger design, and allows life to unfold accordingly; while the dynamic type believes we create our own destiny and that with a strong sense of purpose we can get what we want.

Receptive qualities are opposite to dynamic qualities:

| RECEPTIVE | DYNAMIC |
|---|---|
| Yin | Yang |
| Love | Will |
| Flow | Action |
| "The Grand Design" | Free Will |
| Passive | Aggressive |
| Intuitive | Logical |
| Being | Doing |

People tend either to be one type or the other. If you want to improve your manifestation hit-rate then it's important to establish which one you are at the start, so that you can work toward bringing the opposite type's qualities into your life.

## Receptive Types

You are a receptive type if you:

+ see connections very easily

+ have a tendency to go with the flow

+ are fluid and prefer "being" to "doing"

+ believe everything will work out in the end, that it will be okay and you just have to trust the process

+ hand the outcome over to fate and say that everything is meant to be

Your issue: you see the potential and the possibilities, but have difficulty actualizing them. You lose your way and have no focus.

## Dynamic Types

You are a dynamic type if you:

+ believe you are responsible for what happens

+ believe you can make things happen

+ enjoy challenging yourself and tackling problems

+ feel that solutions come out of making choices

+ like to be in control and know what you're doing at all times

Your Issue: you do everything you can to make things happen, but have difficulty in trusting the universe. You like to be in control and can't hand the delivery over to the cosmos.

In order for the Law of Attraction to work you need to use the qualities of both receiving and acquiring.

If you identify with being *receptive* then you need to be much more active and dynamic in pursuit of your wishes. You need to take practical steps and challenge yourself to make your dreams become reality. Spend more time getting out there into the world and stepping into the unknown, rather than sitting back and waiting for things to come to you in the fullness of time.

If, however, you identify with being more *dynamic*, then you need to work regularly on the visualization techniques above, especially those that help you go with the flow. You need to open yourself to letting go more often and learning how "just be." Remember that you can get what you want simply by staying still rather than chasing after it. The ability to receive is an art which requires a certain level of openness. You need to feel comfortable about receiving.

# HOW WILL YOU KNOW WHEN THE TIME IS RIGHT?

Any change requires an ending and a new beginning. You might be changing something small, like a habit, or you might be tackling a recurring pattern, or in some cases, you might want a radical change that calls for you to give up your old life as you know it.

Any change requires intention, energy, and an act of will so that you can move away from the past and choose to do things differently. If you're trying to change a familiar pattern you need to tell yourself, "I'm not going down that road this time." You need to make an effort. You really have to want to change at a deeper level rather than just thinking it would be nice if it happened. You need to engage your will.

Sometimes you have to let go of something first. Maybe you have to let go of an attachment to an old relationship. Sheila was puzzled about why she never met anybody new when she had been divorced from Mike for 5 years. Yet she never stopped talking about her ex or thinking about him. He was still her main relationship—and her life was full. She needed to clear some space in her head, to put him to one side psychologically in order to make room for someone new to come in. Letting go is not just a thought process, but a true relinquishment or inner full-stop that happens at a pivotal time in your life, and continues to manifest ever after. Being willing implies openness. To go for something new means you have to be ready to do what's right for you and become aware of self-limiting patterns.

❈  ❈  ❈

*You know when the time is right. It's when you arrive at a moment of readiness to try something out.* This is where Jung's theory of synchronicity comes into play. Whatever it is you have in your mind will attract similar energy. For instance, you want to go to a certain place and you bump into somebody who has just come back from there. Or you have an idea and then pick up a book which tells you more about it. Little signals and messages start resonating with what you're trying to do. These are the signposts that say, "Yes, it's the right time for your wish to fall into place."

You then need a flexible outline of how you want things to be. I say flexible, because you are not totally in control. *You are willing for things to change, and you are open to whatever comes along.*

---

# CHAPTER 7

# Desire and Expectation

## SECRETS THAT WILL REVEAL HOW THE LAW OF ATTRACTION CAN HELP A RELATIONSHIP

### YOU ARE WITH SOMEONE AND IT ISN'T WORKING

You can tap into the Law of Attraction when a good relationship is going off the rails. Sometimes you get stuck in a cycle of blips and could use a bit of extra guidance to help pull you out of it. There's no doubt that if you continually focus on problems all you will get is more of the same! Stepping outside of the difficulties and appreciating something positive about the relationship or the other person will immediately bring positive energy into the equation. Letting go of bad feelings is a fabulous step forward. No matter how awful it's been or how badly you feel you've been treated, if you clear out all that toxic energy you'll be doing yourself a huge favor. The more you go over what he or she said or did to you in your mind, the more you'll attract it again. Plugging into good feelings will mean the Law of Attraction can send you something better!

## WHEN WE FEEL COMPELLED TO BE WITH SOMEONE

If you're in the grip of compulsion to be with someone then you're in a spin-cycle, where the universe cannot communicate with you. This is when you feel lost. Lost in an addiction to a person. You want to be with someone, you desire certain things out of the relationship, you expect the person to behave a certain way—you place so much importance on the relationship that it only leads to your feeling let down.

Sometimes it isn't possible to have the person that we want in our lives. They are otherwise engaged, not "right for us," or simply unavailable. We can waste a lot of time in attempting to control the situation: trying to make it happen and to force the other person into doing what we want. But if you understand how the Law of Attraction works you'll be better equipped to let go of an attachment that isn't going to fly. If we can go beyond the limitations of that attachment then we can become open to someone else.

# HOW THE LAW OF ATTRACTION CAN IMPROVE REACTIVE RELATIONSHIPS

You might be in a relationship that feels like a cosmic joke rather than a match made in heaven. At this point, it's easy to lose sight of your connection to the universe. If you are stuck in a reactive relationship, you can't read the signals, find any meaning, get a perspective, or move forward.

First of all you need to look at your relationship. Is it reactive? In other words, does it constantly press the buttons that make you jump into repeat patterns of conflict, without being able to stop yourself? No outside force can break the cycle for you. But if you are ready to stop playing this game with the other person then you can move up a gear and start expecting your experience together to be a happier one.

---

**SYMPTOMS OF A REACTIVE RELATIONSHIP**

+ Are you caught in an ongoing pattern of conflict?

+ Are you constantly dealing with petty fights that take you straight back to the main recurring argument?

+ Do you try to micromanage your partner, so that conflict can be avoided, but find you still fall into the trap?

+ Do you feel as though you are simply surviving in the relationship rather than enjoying it?

+ Have your friends and family advised you to walk away, but you are so hooked in that this feels impossible?

---

When two people are in a relationship where they feel connected on a higher level, then they can simply be, do, and have whatever they want together rather than looking at each other as "the enemy" or experiencing a constant sense of loss and lack.

Any relationship based on a win/lose energy is very black and white, with no shades of grey, and revolves around who is right and who is wrong. The more highly charged the relationship becomes, the more adrenaline is generated between the two of you, and the more caught up in the problem you become.

This kind of relationship has a central theme of possession—where one of you wants either to possess or to be possessed. It is based on the fear that you might run out of time or lose love. When a relationship has these fears at its core, then it's difficult to find any peace with the other person. Fear creates a see-saw of emotions, a pounding of adrenaline, and it prevents us from feeling and receiving love. The compulsion to hang on to that person at all costs is in itself quite a cost. It deprives you of the ability to open up. Clinging to someone is a manifestation of closing down. You are caught in a negative cycle of energy and the universe cannot reach you.

You might think your partner is so stuck that things will never change. How can things change if your partner won't change? But the great news is that he or she doesn't have to! The Law of Attraction stipulates that **it only takes one of**

**you to change and the whole dynamic will re-arrange itself.** So the power to alter the whole set-up is in your hands, because you can change *your* attitude, *your* expectations and *your* beliefs. The minute you drop your expectations, pull out of the power games, and start radiating positive energy the Law of Attraction can send some magic into your life.

## THE BATTLE OF WIN/LOSE

When your relationship is based on a constant diet of fireworks, the adrenaline this produces becomes addictive. You think you are obsessed with the person but in fact, you are addicted to the excitement of the adrenaline rush, which gives you a buzz and is similar to the rush of the "in love" feeling. This person and the dynamic of the relationship triggers a real high. The problem is that it's followed by a real low.

You can become so intoxicated by the ups and downs of the relationship that it's difficult to go cold turkey, which is the only way you will get a balanced perspective. We mistake the drama for love, because it feels so heightened, so passionate. If we are not careful we can convince ourselves it is "so right."

The reality is that a relationship like this is very depleting, and an obsession with a person and with winning makes it impossible to stand back and see things as they really are. If we are totally obsessed with someone then we cut ourselves off from any other possibilities. The result is that emotionally we become out of balance and damaged from living in a state of constant tension.

---

**THE TOXIC BLOCKS TO RELATING**

Do we have any power over what happens in our relationships? We always do, although sometimes we may need to reclaim it.

Does the universe send us the kind of people who can teach us a thing or two? Yes. We imagine things should be perfect between us and our partner, but usually we learn the most from difficulties.

Sometimes we get so caught up in our toxic blocks that the relationship gets really and truly stuck. That's when we need to dig deep inside to discover why it's happened.

---

## THE CINDERELLA COMPLEX

This is a very common trap. It means we are dependent on another person to feel good about ourselves, and we only see ourselves reflected in their eyes. This is dangerous because it means we are not building up a strong inner core, we have low self-esteem and lack the ability to feel okay, either with or without the other person.

In some cases, you might project your destiny on to someone else, so that they seemingly have the power to determine the outcome of your life. You remain small, and your life is permanently on hold as you wait for *them* to make all the decisions. You wait for them to decide, for instance, if they are going to commit.

Letting go of the image of yourself as Cinderella can be surprisingly hard. The fairy tale dynamic will have to come to an end, and the illusion must be dealt with, as you try to meet life on more realistic terms. Dropping the role of Cinderella means taking responsibility for your own life and realizing that you can do something about what's going on, that you can't just blame others.

---

One very important component of the Law of Attraction is that we can only create the lives we want when there is no one else to blame! In other words, if we blame someone else, then we are powerless—because they are in control, and we automatically lose the power to change things. The moment we stop blaming others, we stop harming ourselves and gain the freedom to create something better.

---

# THE GAME OF PING-PONG

There you are in your relationship, with the arguments flying back and forth. There is one level where this is healthy and another where it is toxic. You will instinctively know the difference between them. The toxic argument is ongoing and it can be triggered by small things, but it quickly gets deep beneath your skin. It is characterized by a simmering resentment and a continual battle which both people in the relationship are struggling to win.

It always takes two people to create a problem. There is some kind of unconscious pact to play a game that keeps the issue going on and on, both parties batting it between them like a well-rehearsed game of ping-pong. It is self perpetuating, yet it only takes one person to change it.

To make the change happen you need to step outside of the known parameters and stop the destructive behavior. You have to approach this with a genuine willingness to do things differently, and not be half-hearted. You might think you don't play games, but you do. This ongoing battle/ pattern/conflict is, in fact, a game. And if there is going to be any change then you need to take responsibility for your own part in it. What are you doing to keep it going? What are the moves you make, the thoughts you think, and the things you say?

The game of ping-pong is often triggered by arguments that start over something relatively small. There's so much that overlays the real and deeper issues that we think we're arguing about X, when really it's Y that's the problem. There's a reality behind the reality. Recognizing what it is this person is triggering within you is a vital step toward dealing with it.

With such an ingrained pattern between the two of you, you have to do more than just dream or desire that things were different. You need to muster up every ounce of motivation and *be willing for it to be different.* It's so easy to slip back into the game of ping pong, because it feels familiar and it gives the payoff of feeling that you are right and they are wrong.

**QUESTIONS TO ASK YOURSELF ABOUT THE GAME
OF PING-PONG**

+ How am I keeping it going?

+ Do I think of somebody in a particular way, and then find that he or she conforms to my view of them?

+ Am I willing to let go of the conflict I have with this person?

+ What do I get out of the game? (Being right, enjoying the drama, venting my stress, enjoying the challenge?)

+ Can I let go of wanting something from this person?

+ What is the conflict really about for me?

+ Do I have the desire, belief, and expectancy that things can change?

# REVIEW THE GAME AND YOUR MINDSET

If we think of someone in a certain way then he or she will *be* that way—for us. Obviously other people will have different views of them and will experience them from different angles. Yet we continually keep someone stuck by seeing them through our own personal lens. We box them in. *However, we can change the world by changing our perception.*

If you accept people as they are, without insisting they change, you are creating the possibility of something new happening—the Law of Attraction will respond to your positive new outlook.

# CLEARING THE EMOTIONAL ISSUES

Become aware of what it is you're holding on to, whether it be blame, guilt, resentment, or anything else. You are the one who is suffering as a result of harboring these feelings. They attach themselves to your emotional body and clog up your psyche, creating a heavy, impenetrable, and in some cases, bitter feeling. Letting go of this bad stuff will free up your whole energy. But you can't just pay lip service to the idea of being free of it—you really have to *want* to clear it up.

> You can ask the universe to help you become free of these feelings. But don't ask it to change the other person, because it's not the responsibility of the universe to do so.

People who have high self-esteem are automatically less threatened by whatever anyone else says. You can cultivate higher self esteem by "acting as if" you have it. You can begin by thinking, "No matter what you say, I'm not going to feel threatened." As Eleanor Roosevelt once observed, "No one can make me feel inferior without my consent."

> You can ask the universe for help in feeling better about yourself, and in letting go of any of those "not good enough" messages that may lurk inside you.

# HOW CAN THE UNIVERSE HELP?

Can you look beyond the behavior of the other person and see what is happening between the two of you? Try seeing the reason why the person is behaving like this. Someone's childish behavior is just that—the small child inside them that wants their own way or is having a tantrum, it's not the adult that's standing in front of you. Instead of focusing on their bad behavior you can try seeing this person as a soul with a rather difficult personality who's not doing what we want! There is more to this person than them being a walking argument waiting to happen! If you expand your awareness, taking into account the other person's neuroses, fears, attachments, insecurities, needs, desires, and wants, then you create a position where at least you can step back. If we could just stop wanting to wipe out the part of their personality we don't like, but rather include it (without judgment if possible), this means we can move on, even if we remain in the relationship.

---

**We don't have to like or agree with what they say or do, but it helps if we can accept them as a person. You can ask the universe for help with this acceptance, because although you may not be able to change this person, you can change yourself.**

---

# TECHNIQUE FOR SEEING DEEP INSIDE THE ISSUE

The next exercise helps you see how the other person is thinking, what drives them, and how you appear to them! Place two chairs opposite each other, with a cushion on the floor in between. One will be your chair and one will represent the other person. Sit in your own chair and visualize the other person sitting opposite you. Recall the tension that exists between you. Perhaps you don't feel comfortable with this person, or they irritate you, or the difficulties between you prevent you from feeling generous toward them. If it helps, write down what the difficulty is from your point of view, explaining how you feel about it.

Now switch chairs. Visualize yourself as the other person. Try to imagine what it's like to be them: what you look like to them, how you present yourself, and how you feel. Exaggerate. Make some statements that they might make: I am X, I feel X, I think X, I defend myself by X. Become them as you look at yourself in the other chair, and notice what they see and how they feet about you. Now imagine having their dreams, hopes, and fears. Really take them on board. What are they about? How do they make you behave? Write down any insights if you wish.

Now become neutral by dissociating yourself from either person and from the problem. Sit on the cushion in between the two chairs. Are you able to see from here anything more about this issue or the real needs of the two people involved? What drives them and what needs to happen for the pattern to be broken or a better understanding to emerge? Write down any insights.

Doing this exercise helps us to see our *projections.* All along, we have looked at the other person from our own point of view. By *becoming them* we suddenly realize how it actually feels to *be them.* Projection is something we all do, most of the time, because it is so difficult to be transparent and to see others clearly. We make personal judgments, comments, and decisions about other people which are based on our own values. We even view them as people who behave in a way that we would "never do." Yet this is because we have repressed an aspect of ourselves that is still lurking in the undergrowth of our psyche. Any time that we get a charge of energy around a particular person, it's a signal that something about them is connecting to something in us.

## STOP PLAYING THE GAME

We can choose how we respond to others. We can choose to remain serene and have a handle on things, if that is what we wish.

**You can practice responding, rather than reacting, by:**

+ taking the time to allow a plan, an idea, or a response to come together slowly

+ breaking a habit

+ taking a risk and doing something that is outside your comfort zone

*Start implementing these tools in your relationship.*

# LETTING GO OF PAST RELATIONSHIPS

It's easy to continue our attachment to somebody long after the relationship is technically over. We can carry a torch for someone, we compare other people to them, we become nostalgic for the good times we had together. Or we continually replay the bad times in our minds, thereby maintaining the history in the present. The person is a ghostlike presence in our lives, and so much of our emotional psychic energy is stuck to them that there is little available for anybody new.

**Tackling your unfinished business is vital (even if you do it on your own). Ask yourself:**

+ What is it that I can't let go of?

+ What am I holding on to?

+ How does this prevent me from getting on with the rest of my life?

+ Do I still long for this person? Why?

+ Is this the only person in the world with the quality I long for?

+ What didn't I say to them?

+ What didn't I do?

+ What prevents me from resolving this?

+ Can I accept and allow this relationship to be finished, and can I achieve a state of peace within myself?

All you have to do is work on your own bit of unfinished business.

# TECHNIQUE FOR LETTING GO OF SOMEONE

Imagine you are standing in one half of a figure of eight. The person you are trying to let go of is standing in the other half. You are joined together, but separate. Place anything that belongs to you within your own circle and anything that belongs to them in theirs, including words, events, possessions, and experiences. Gradually you can see the two circles moving away from one another, separating into two complete and individual units.

# CHAPTER 8

# It's Up to You

One of the most exciting secrets of the Law of Attraction is that so much of life really is up to you. Okay, things will happen that you didn't wish for—fate decrees that certain elements come into your life, but after that it's up to you! You are free to do whatever you want with life. We make of it what we will. We can choose to go on playing with opportunities, engaging with life, putting out our desires and intentions, and staying positive.

## THE KEY INGREDIENTS

### WHAT ARE YOU LOOKING FOR?

First of all, it's very important to become conscious of what exactly you are looking for. Don't be vague. Stop letting the old patterns play out in your life. Start actively looking instead of day-dreaming.

### CAN YOU TRUST?

Check out how cynical you are. Do you believe in the power of the Law of Attraction? Can you place your trust in something higher, in some kind of divine wisdom, guidance, and meaning? Being able to look the cosmos in the eye and have the nerve to state your dearest wishes requires faith in life. Faith isn't automatic. If you work on developing your intuition, and if you believe in the wisdom and meaning of life, then you are forming a connection with the unseen. It means letting go of any skeptical attitude and protecting yourself from other people's cynicism. It's so easy to doubt, to mock. *Its so easy to close down. But closing down won't get you anywhere.* It will just make everything smaller and place restrictions on what is available to you.

Being able to take life on, to engage with it instead of being a bystander, requires courage and energy. You either sit back and let life happen to you, or you really start living. If you can get your energy flowing you'll find you can attract love, do the things you want, sort out your problems, help other people, feel healthier, make more money, and feel more satisfied. Life will feel so much better, which means it's a win-win situation.

So it's important to trust in life, even if at times you can't understand what's happening or why. Practice receiving what's coming, even if it's not quite what you want...yet. Hold the intention without expectation, and wait without struggling. Say to yourself that you're relaxing into life.

## REALIZE IT'S ALL THERE FOR YOU

The most important thing is to *stop panicking*. We feel there must be a deadline for having what we want, but universal timing works purely on its own terms. Being graceful, poised, and elegant means you can handle anything. Relax from the tension of having to have everything now (just like a screaming toddler). You're getting the best there is available at the time. Being grateful is also good news. Otherwise we are caught in a cycle of wanting more and more, and never appreciating what we already have.

The premise of abundant thinking is that there is no shortage. There's always enough, and if you're experiencing delay it's because you're creating one through your thoughts and actions.

The more desperate you are, the more stuck the energy becomes. Desperation is a repelling force. And if you play hard to get then you're blocking off ways for the delivery to get through. *Focus on being warm, anticipatory, and relaxed*. That magnetic energy of affinity and attraction works best when you are desirable, so realize that you are and be it!

Once you understand that there is a connection between what is happening to you on the outside and what is going on within you, then you've really got a fantastic tool to play with. Practice with it at first on the small things: intending and imagining a happy day, a parking space, a good meeting, the clothing size you want being in stock. Always affirm what you want—not what you don't want.

Then on a larger scale, when it comes to magnetizing a relationship, this tool will give you the power to change your pattern. You will see that the threat or the opportunity is *in you* and not out there after all. You can start choosing to be what you want and to stop behaving automatically.

# DEVELOP YOUR PERSONAL AWARENESS

## RELEASE THE TENSION

A Buddhist monk once taught me the importance of doing "Living Meditations." We don't need to adopt special poses or perform rituals to get in touch with the power of reflection. We can go outside and just look up into the night sky. See ourselves as a mere speck in the universe and recognize that there is more to life than our problems. We can walk by a river and let the flow of the water soothe us as we realize that "this too will pass."

We can also breathe properly and calm down. When you hold on to your breath your whole system starts to shut down. Simply by breathing deeply and evenly we can get back into the flow, the connection between taking in and letting out. You can cleanse and clear yourself of any bad feelings, and effect a huge letting go by breathing out your internal toxic energy in a big whoosh of breath. Feel the release in your body and let the tension drop away.

---

It's easy to forget how much choice we have over how we feel at any given moment.

+ We can't choose what happens to us all the time, but we can always choose how we respond.

+ We have so many thoughts, memories, and "things to do" buzzing around in our minds that we feel fragmented and exhausted. Clearing the chatter in our heads is vital for being effective in realizing our desires and internal well-being.

The way you carry yourself is a dead giveaway of what's going on inside you. It also transmits huge messages to others.

---

**BODILY GIVEAWAYS**

+ Not looking someone in the eye—conveys a lack of connection

+ A knee constantly vibrating up and down indicates nervous energy or impatience

+ Hunched shoulders—shows a need for self-protection or a feeling of being burdened

+ Looking rigid—means you are uptight or tense

---

**OPENING UP AND CLOSING DOWN**

Imagine you are a flower. First visualize yourself as a closed bud, holding all your color, perfume, and glory inside you. Then slowly imagine yourself opening up into a flower; notice each petal unfold. When you are at full stretch enjoy the feeling of being radiantly open and available for all to see. You are in your prime. Then watch the petals slowly close up again, one by one, until you are back to being a tight bud. You have complete control over when to open and when to close. Practice!

To be able to stay emotionally open requires you to be open in your body and your mind. But what about protecting ourselves? We don't want to be sitting targets for someone else's negative energy. You can practice opening up and closing down with this simple visualization.

## OUR CHOICES

We can *choose to see our projections*—where we super-impose ourselves (usually the parts we don't want to acknowledge) on to someone else. *That person is mean, tricky, and so on.* We attribute our unconscious desires and impulses to someone else. Once we realize that our perception of whether something is positive or negative is up to us, then we don't need to spend our time and energy in judging the other person, but are able to get on with our own lives. It's all a projection anyway and we can decide either way—and then we've got a lot more power over our lives.

We can *choose to see a crisis as an opportunity.* The Chinese word for crisis is *wei-chi,* which joins together the concept of crisis and opportunity. We may have a problem on our hands, but if we insist on viewing it as a difficulty then we will lose out on the opportunity that's contained within it. *In the end it's not what actually happens to us, but what we think about what happens to us that counts.*

We can *choose to intend* to attract what we want and do something positive about it. By the way, procrastination is the opposite of intention.

We can *choose to stay connected* to the cosmos, to ourselves, and to each other. Or remember that we are all connected. Energy itself is connected, however random and chaotic it seems, so that scientists have even pondered whether a butterfly flapping its wings in Texas could set off a typhoon in Tokyo six days later. But this sense of connection is nothing new. "All things by immortal power, hiddenly linked to each other are, For thou can't stir of a flower without the troubling of a star." (Francis Thompson)

We can *choose to travel light*: "Dance like nobody's watching, love like you've never been hurt, sing like nobody's listening, live like it's heaven on earth." (Mark Twain)

We can *choose to accept.* Acceptance gives you the most power to do anything you want. It is the pivot and is surprisingly dynamic. It does not mean that you have to forget—or that you agree—with someone's behavior or something that's happened. But the act of acceptance contains magical potency. It means that internally you can change and rearrange your own reactions and live life in a state of peacefulness. Sometimes *(but don't count on it!)* the whole situation gets transformed.

## RAISE YOUR ENERGY LEVELS

Occasionally we talk about it being "one of those days," when nothing seems to go right. Or of being "on a roll," when seemingly we can do nothing wrong. Whatever the cause of this, whether it's a run of luck, difficult energy, static interference, a series of mishaps stemming from carelessness, or a string of opportunities that all come together, we are realizing that the timing is either right or wrong and that we can work with it.

Making yourself aware of when it's not the right time means you can conserve energy and direct it to where you can make best use of it. For instance, if you try and make a phone call to a certain person or organization several times but find you're not getting through—either they are constantly engaged or are unavailable—then this is a message from the universe. Leave it! You will only waste time and energy if you continue trying to make that call. If you wait until another day you'll often find that you get through right away. You might choose to be *dynamic* and keep plugging away, in the Donald Trump modus operandi, but this is really your ego trying to assert its superiority over the universal flow of energy. Alternatively, you might choose to be *receptive* to the signals. To do something else with your time and wait until the weak energy is strengthened and starts to flow again. It's all a chain reaction—one thing leads to another and we rush around attracting more bad things.

You can get what you want by being still.

The same goes for when you're out shopping for something. No matter where you go or what you try on it isn't quite right, doesn't look good on you, or they don't have it in your size. You can pick this up very quickly if it happens twice in a row. Abandon your shopping trip, unless you want to drive yourself crazy and waste time. As you open up your energy you'll quickly read what's in the atmosphere. Whether there's an energy low or an energy high, you will read the signals and get the message. If you can start the day by imagining how you want it to go, then you're half way there to attracting the right energy. Take a few minutes before you even get out of bed to gather your thoughts and visualize what you want to achieve. That's far better than starting off in an unconscious state and letting events control you.

We are so used to being stressed, to having "the buzz," that we lose the ability to be still. So much emphasis is placed on "being busy" that only extrovert activity gains any kudos in our twenty-first-century mind set. In fact, we now wear our stress like a badge of honor to show how important, needed, busy, and successful we are. Then, when we do finally have some time off, our bodies are unable to relax. Actually it takes a lot more energy to be uptight than it does to be relaxed. Being so busy steals and saps our energy. And it robs us of a still place where we can connect to the universe.

Of course, energy responds well to a better diet and a cleaner, tidier, quieter environment. We are addicted to media, to being "in touch" with each other through impersonal means such as texting. Bombarding each other and becoming invaded by shocking media headlines depletes our pure energy. If we constantly soak up bad news on television, read mindless trash, and gossip about people, then our good energy gets depleted. Just be aware of what's going on in your environment. You can use Feng shui to clear your space.

---

**THE VOID SPACE**

Sometimes we're thrown into a void space. The subway train is stuck in the tunnel, the bus won't come, the person we're meeting is running late. This is not a waste of time! These are opportunities to go into the void and mentally rebalance, or reconnect with what we want—and then put out a few wishes. The extra time is a powerful gift that you can use to create the future you want. And the beauty of the Law of Attraction for Love is that you can tap into it anywhere at any time.

---

# AND FINALLY

We are all searchers looking for someone or something to make us feel complete. So often we imagine another person will make us feel this way, but we can really only find this feeling from within. And the mere mention of "finding it within" can make us feel empty, as we mentally check our stomach cavities and realize that all that's in there is a can of baked beans, or some Goji berries (if we're the healthy sort), but certainly not an eternal and abundant supply of bliss and happiness. So where is this bliss? Ancient Taoist wisdom talks about "the source" from which all things come and to which all things return. Everything comes from here, whether it's a handbag, a hot dog, or a happy smile. Being able to access this place is your ticket to happiness. And the more frequently you go there, partake of it, and bring it into your life, the happier you will be. No matter what happens. Being able to connect with that vast floating abundance is your chance to recharge, and it's the closest thing to heaven available on earth. It is your permanently available source of security—and you can plug into it at any time. *It's up to you!*

# About the Author

**Debbie Frank** pens the astrology sections of the *Daily Mirror*, the *Sunday Mirror*, and *First* magazine. Debbie has been an astrologer for more than twenty years, and she supported Princess Diana through the last eight traumatic years of her life. Debbie's a Scorpio and lives in London with her husband and daughter.

Visit her website at www.debbiefrank.co.uk.